THE HOPE OF

CW00820330

A Chaplain's Journey to Al
Enduring Hope and Love Under Fire

Copyright 2024 © Larry D. Cripps

Emissary

Published in Phoenix, Arizona by Emissary Publishing.
Emissary is a business trade name of Ed's Voices, LLC.

Scripture quotations are taken from the NIV Bible (The Holy Bible, New International Version), copyright 1978 by Biblica Ministries, a nonprofit Bible and publishing ministry.

DEDICATION

To My Parents

Freddie "Hoyte" and Naomi Sue (Underwood) Cripps

Their influence led me to Christ and ignited
my passion for life and ministry.

To My Wife

Charlene Ann (Yates) Cripps

She is the source of joy and inspiration
that fuels my life and ministry.

To my Children, Grandchildren, and Great Grandchildren

My greatest treasures in life, who inspire me to strive
for excellence and remind me every day
of my true purpose and legacy.

TABLE OF CONTENTS

IN MEMORIAM

PFC Alvin Dale Hutchings, USMC
CPL Ronnie Ellis Reader, USMC
PFC B. L. Murphy Jr., USMC
SP/4 Danny Stephen Young, USA
PFC Billy Anthony Adcock, USA
MSGT Robert Lewis Bolan, USA
SP/4 Neal Vincent Bainter, USA
SGT William Lester Wilhelm, USA
PVT Joseph Frank Marcantonio, USA
CPT Carl Lynn West, USA
WO1 John Henry Cannon, USA
SP/5 Allen Carson Hardison, USA
SP/5 Robert James Oates, USA
CPT Kendrick King Kelley III, USA

Blackhorse Troopers Killed in Vietnam
September 1966—April 1972

11th Armored Cavalry South Vietnamese Scouts
Young men who sacrificed everything in the service of their country

Admired Friend and Mentor
CPT Stan Corvin, Jr., USA

Beloved Young Men Taken Much Too Soon
Zachary Estes
Wayne G. Cripps
Erie R. Hendrix
James "Jim" A. Rhody
Roger Estes
Edward Frazier
G. Patrick Vincion
Lee Hendrix

Against all hope, Abraham in hope believed and so became the father of many nations, just as it had been said to him, "So shall your offspring be." Without weakening in his faith, he faced the fact that his body was as good as dead – since he was about a hundred years old – and that Sarah's womb was also dead. Yet he did not waver through unbelief regarding the promise of God, but was strengthened in his faith and gave glory to God, being fully persuaded that God had the power to do what he had promised.
Romans 4:18-21

Foreword

In the early 1990s, I commanded the U.S. Navy's Naval Mobile Construction Battalion TWENTY FOUR (NMCB-24). I habitually paid close attention to our sailors' conditions, usually by gathering data and insights from staff members I could trust. One of the most important people I counted on in particular for unvarnished answers was the chaplain.

We were a Navy Reserve "Seabee" battalion—one of the Navy's troop construction units. During my time in command, we served overseas in Operations Desert Shield and Desert Storm. While our unit's regular chain of command always had some sense of sailors' morale and welfare, it tended to filter and qualify that information.

The chaplain was different.

Larry Cripps, a lieutenant commander at the time, served as the chaplain for our Seabees. Larry was one of our "special staff"— officers and enlisted sailors with specialized, professional education and experience. The size and challenges of managing our unit (over 750 total personnel assigned) made these positions vital to our success.

I first met Larry in the fall of 1989. He impressed me with his energy and passion for his "job" as chaplain. I put "job" in quotation marks because, in Larry's case, chaplaincy was far more than a job; it was his calling. First and foremost, he was motivated to serve our battalion, helping Seabees to be the best they could be as they carried out their missions. His actions always aligned with his words.

The second thing that impressed me was Larry's extensive, varied background. He brought an authentic, authoritative perspective to our discussions and meetings. Anytime he came to me and said, "We have to talk," I learned that it was wise to stop what I was doing and listen.

We spent two years together in NMCB-24, including eight months of pre-deployment training and operational deployment in Saudi Arabia and Kuwait for Desert Storm. Larry refused to sit behind a desk during the week and preach on Sundays. He wanted to be "out with the troops" wherever they were—project sites, training ranges, classrooms, or on the battlefield. He worked hard to make himself available for all our sailors, to listen and offer counsel.

Between the start of the air and ground wars in Desert Storm, our battalion spread out in fourteen different locations. We ranged from a three-person detachment with Navy Special Operations to a reinforced air detachment of 120 Seabees at King Abdul Aziz Air Base and a "Main Element" of two hundred Seabees on the Kuwait border with the Marines' Direct Support Command. Working within our operational and security constraints, Larry never sat still; he insisted on visiting as many sailors as possible.

Wherever he went, Larry gathered insight into how our sailors were really doing and shared his assessments with me, even if they were uncomfortable. He discreetly respected the line between general and personal/confidential information, but he wasn't afraid to tell me what he thought. As a result I felt genuinely well-informed on our sailors' morale and readiness, and because of that, I could often anticipate issues before they arose.

Describing my experience working with Larry sets the stage for what you're about to read. He *always* had valuable stories to share, even back then. His passion for service, common sense approach, and God-centered focus drove him to confront his own internal challenges. They fueled his mission to help others find the same kind of hope. When it's time for a real-life physical battle, few things are more valuable than a clear mind and a calm soul. Larry wants those things for everyone.

You'll find value in Larry's emphasis on teamwork and personal relationships. I remember it so well; as I look back, I see how he, along with our Command Master Chief, was part of a "1-2 punch" advisory team every leader should have. Few leaders follow through on finding those advisors; it's little wonder leadership is such a rocky road without them. I was blessed; I had an abundance of honest counsel, especially from the chaplain.

Larry champions the spirit of service. I've never known him any other way, even now, decades after we finished our military careers. He is passionate about being "in the mix" wherever there's an opportunity to contribute to others. This book manifests his desire to see people set free and flourishing. He may be in the fourth quarter of life, but he's nowhere near "finished."

The Hope of War is autobiographical. You'll read about Larry's decades of service and a heartfelt description of his struggles to grow into his calling and future.

But it's also a field manual for living through and learning from your experiences and seeking and applying God's truth in practical ways. While combat and the "school of hard knocks" certainly accelerated Larry's learning, these principles can be used anywhere, anytime… and you don't need to wear a military uniform.

Larry deeply desires for people to find meaning in their struggles and experiences. Beginning with Vietnam, he reminds us to mobilize whatever goodness and truth we can find, no matter where God calls or sends us. If you feel "lost at sea," Larry's stories provide navigational beacons for the soul. Few feelings are worse for a sailor than being lost at sea without navigational aids; few give you more hope than finding your bearings, the sight of land, or friendly ships on the horizon.

I had the privilege of reading Larry's manuscript as he developed it. It caused several wheels to turn for me, some of which had not moved for a long time. I could connect details of my past to the feelings, experiences, and principles he shares. If you've ever felt "stuck" on the inside, with conflict and emotions that seem random or unrelated to the present... think again. Like your body, your soul gives off "pain" signals. Larry's stories will help you re-evaluate them and seek help to overcome them so you can leave a legacy for future generations to build on.

It's an honor to contribute to this book. I'm even more excited about the hope Larry found because I know what it can do for you. We all live through "messes," but few of us ever find the "message" God leaves in the rubble. Larry is among those happy few. It's my hope you take the opportunity to read, take action, and join him among those ranks.

James M. (Jim) McGarrah
Rear Admiral, Civil Engineer Corps
United States Navy (Ret.)

THE HOPE OF WAR

Introduction

It was April 1971. I was seated in a Boeing 707 as it taxied along the tarmac at Bien Hoa Air Base in South Vietnam at what felt like a snail's pace. I kept thinking, "The enemy could easily fire a single mortar round and take us all out in one fell swoop."

After our plane turned onto the end of the runway, the pilot gunned the engines, hurling the aircraft ever faster down the runway. As its nose lifted into the air, all on board let loose with shouts of joy, knowing that our life in Vietnam's hot, treacherous jungles lay behind us on the ground below. We were on our way home and toward all things familiar. If only we'd understood how much our lives had changed, that "home" would never be the same again.

It feels like a lifetime has passed since I was in Vietnam, but memories of the war still linger. As soon as I hear the distinct whopping sound of helicopter blades in the distance or smell something putrid, my mind drifts back to Vietnam. I hear soldiers shouting over gunfire and injured men screaming in agony. When mosquitoes buzz in my ear on a hot, humid day in my home state of Tennessee, I feel like I'm back at Bien Hoa. Even the silence sometimes reminds me of Vietnam, for just when we thought it was quiet enough to say something, another explosion ripped through the air.

I received my draft notice in the spring of 1969. During the Vietnam War, every young man over eighteen understood we had a chance of being called up. By the time I entered the U.S. Army in August, three high school friends and an uncle had already been killed in Vietnam. The previous June, *Life* Magazine shocked the nation when it published the names and photos of 242 men killed in Vietnam during a week of fighting. It was a reminder of the human toll the war exacted. The media released a steady stream of gripping photographs and films beginning in 1965, but none of it struck me the same way as the names and pictures of all those young men who perished in a single week of fighting.

I still remember the sadness that gripped my heart, knowing these young men would never get the chance to raise families and pursue their dreams. Instead, their hopes for the future were gone, leaving their families with only memories and lingering thoughts of what might have been. A great many of my generation spent a lot of time wondering what might have been.

Early on, the American public supported our involvement in Vietnam. We believed it was essential to stop the spread of communism in Southeast Asia. Morale among American troops was high, but as the war dragged on, it deteriorated. By 1969, the confidence and performance of U.S. military forces was the lowest it had ever been. As American casualties increased, some soldiers became frustrated that there was no end in sight. Others grew exasperated with Washington's lack of a coherent war strategy, which seemed to risk our lives on endless patrols… without a plan for victory or closure.

Another reason for declining morale and performance was Vietnam's one-year tour-of-duty rotation schedule. In previous wars, U.S. troops were required to serve for the duration of the conflict. You might have spent three or four years with some close friends, fighting side-by-side. However, in Vietnam, individual combat soldiers were rotated into and out of the country on a one-year schedule. Most of us focused mainly on staying alive until the end of our tour of duty rather than fighting to the end of the conflict. With an undefined mission, no clear path to victory, and a maximum of 365 days' participation—this conflict was very different from existential, must-win battles like World War II.

I remember lengthy periods of "hurry up and wait" and extreme boredom, mixed with interruptions of sudden, unexpected terror. But once I reached the halfway point of the tour, I began marking off the days on a calendar I drew on the lid of a C-ration box. When I returned home, I tried to forget the monotony, boredom, mosquitoes, and sweltering heat. But I've never forgotten those moments of sheer terror. After all these years, I still occasionally dream about them. As the years turned to decades, I had a lot of time to think about my experience. Events like the terrorist attacks on September 11th, 2001, forced me to remember and process the past. I realized some of those memories never truly healed because I was unwilling to admit they'd impacted me, to begin with.

American soldiers grew disillusioned over Vietnam, and some began to vent their frustrations on officers. Most officers were respectable leaders who earned their soldiers' admiration. But some placed their desire for recognition ahead of the safety and welfare of their men. We resented officers who directed combat operations from the safety of high-flying helicopters or distant command posts. We also disliked overly aggressive officers who refused to listen to the advice of experienced, non-commissioned officers (NCOs). We began to see them as "reinforcements" of an unspoken mission nobody could explain. No one seemed to know why we were in Vietnam, even at the highest levels of command. But it was too late to turn back; we had to keep going.

Many people asked questions like "What could have been?" about Vietnam for years after it officially ended in 1975. "Why did we go? What did we hope to accomplish there? What did we learn from a decade-long war? Did we learn anything?" Unfortunately, the answers eluded us in the jungles, hamlets, and mountainous regions of Vietnam.

As time passed, attitudes about the war softened. The government declassified many of its documents for study. Today, many people revisit memories of the war that were too raw to talk about at the time. They're searching for a semblance of "truth" about Vietnam. I'm hopeful you'll find some of it in the pages of this book. Many questions that came up for me during those days have been answered. I'm pleased to say the answers were there all along; I simply wasn't ready to hear them.

An ancient philosopher once said, "There is no single truth in war, for we are all prisoners of our own experience." If there's one thing standing in the way of the search for truth, it's that each person experienced Vietnam just a little differently from the next. Some look back on it with anger, resentment, and inconsolable grief. Others remember it with confusion, like an unresolved equation circling forever in the recesses of their minds. Some remember it with honor and pride and treasured stories of comradeship and heroism. Some remember it as little more than an exotic vacation.

If you were to ask me the truth of the Vietnam War and whether it was worth the cost we paid to participate, I'd answer: "It depends on how you look at it."

Everyone knows how precarious life can be. Tragedy and loss strike without warning, accidents happen, and unforeseen circumstances disrupt the best-laid plans of mice and men. We might do everything within our power to prevent such things. We may even tell ourselves, "What happened to others will never happen to me."

But in Vietnam, we quickly learned that "a good day" could mean many things: patrolling in the jungle without stepping on a landmine, being wounded but escaping life-threatening injuries, or being directly next to the man tagged "killed in action" by the medic. Death is your constant companion in war, and near misses are everyday occurrences. Combat in Vietnam gave us a broader category of "a good day" and taught us to appreciate the tiniest, most insignificant shreds of "goodness" we could find.

The principal architects of the Vietnam conflict never envisioned any of this. They couldn't foresee how bitterly divisive the war would become. Of course, there were plenty of wrong things about the war. But as time passed, I began to understand how much goodness came from it... if you knew where to look. It is a goodness that cannot be purchased or inherited; you can only acquire it by letting yourself get swept up into something much bigger than yourself.

I went to Vietnam without understanding why—at least, from an eternal point of view. I thought I'd simply gone to do a difficult, dirty job: thwart communist aggression and expansion in Southeast Asia. It didn't occur to me then that by answering the call of duty, I also answered a much larger calling. I didn't understand that the God of the Bible doesn't need unanimous public support or the approval of the international community to do incredible work in a person's life. He's comfortable working in environments like Vietnam, onboard an aircraft carrier, or in the Pentagon after 9/11. God doesn't need "paradise" conditions in the heart of a believer to unlock new levels of maturity, obedience, and relationship with Him. But when believers embrace how He works, it's amazing how often paradise conditions show up... even in war zones.

That's why I call this book *The Hope of War*. I believe whether you fought alongside my generation or you're currently serving, whether you believe in God or not, whether you serve(d) as a warrior or a family member...

Everyone needs help maintaining perspective.

Everyone needs a reason to continue believing when things seem hopeless.

Everyone needs to know there was courage, dignity, and meaning in the work they did... even things that seemed utterly meaningless.

Everyone needs to hear the truth.

If you were in Vietnam with us, the truth is that you haven't "blown it." You're not "going under." Your effort wasn't a waste, and the story is not over.

If anything, it's the other way around. Your story is still being written, and you have tremendous influence over how it ends... if you're willing to believe it.

If you're young and serving today... it's simply your turn to discover what some of us older warriors already know.

If you're a family member serving alongside a warrior, my prayer is that you find comfort and clarity in understanding the journey of the person you love. Both you and they walk a road most people will never truly understand.

But whatever you are, it's time to step into God's calling on your life. To activate it and walk it out. Don't be surprised if you need to spend time in a spiritual combat zone yourself. In God's Kingdom, that's where the victories happen.

You might need to go to an environment where you're forced to appreciate the tiniest fragments of joy and hope you can find.

For all I know, you might be in a combat zone right now. If you're my age, you might have been there… and never really left.

None of that matters now. It's time to start your journey to the abiding faith, enduring hope, and love under fire that only war zones can provide.

May you find the joy that such a journey can bring.

Larry D. Cripps

Chapter One
The People and the Place

We should never take our background for granted. Whether good or bad, God will use whatever we lay at His feet for purposes greater than we can imagine.

"Between the stimulus and response, there is a space. And in that space lies our freedom and power to choose our responses. In our response lies our growth and our freedom."

- Dr. Viktor Frankl, *Man's Search for Meaning*

My hometown of Smithville in Middle Tennessee overflows with history, dating back to the 18th century. DeKalb County, where the city is located, is named after Johann DeKalb, a German general who served in the Continental Army during the American Revolutionary War. The name "Smithville" honors the life and service of Samuel Gainville Smith, a Jackson County resident who served as a state senator and secretary of state. Culturally, Middle Tennessee is considered part of the "Upland South," which depended on migrant settlers and enslaved African Americans to cultivate commodity crops, such as cotton and tobacco, during the Antebellum Era. Planters also bred and trained livestock, such as the world-famous Tennessee walking horse, which was developed as a breed in the region.[1]

During the American Civil War, the Union Army occupied Tennessee from 1862 until the end of the war. Battles and campaigns occurred across the state, and almost every county witnessed combat. Some of the most intense fighting happened along the Tennessee and Cumberland Rivers, which the Union and the Confederacy regarded as key strategic waterways. The same went for mountain passes, such as the Cumberland Gap. The Battle of Stones River, fought between December 31, 1862, and January 2, 1864, near Murfreesboro, was one of the war's bloodiest engagements. Those skirmishes yielded significant military and political gains for the Union and left an indelible mark on the nation's collective memory.[2]

Tennessee was the last Southern state to secede from the Union, and its people were sharply divided on the issue of secession. Some Eastern counties, for example, harbored pro-Union sentiments throughout the conflict. DeKalb County offered up almost as many troops to one side as they did to the other. My great-grandfather, Zenith (Zene) Cripps, and his older brother, Thomas, were loyal Unionists, living among neighbors and friends who held equally strong sentiments for Southern sovereignty. Zene and Thomas were teenagers when they enlisted in the Union Army in the spring of 1863. Subsequently, they were assigned to the 5th Tennessee Cavalry Regiment, an all-volunteer unit under Colonel William Brickly Stokes, a prominent lawyer and participant in local and state politics.[3]

My ancestors saw action in some of the state's most ferocious battles. They were at the Battle of Stones River in Murfreesboro and part of what was known as the Tullahoma Campaign. They fought at Missionary Ridge in Chattanooga and Chickamauga, which lay across the state line in North Georgia. Tennessee was strategically significant to Union forces because it was a border state with numerous key waterways, giving them easy access to the deeper South. As a result, the Union controlled all the transportation routes and mountain passes into neighboring states like North Carolina and Kentucky. Except for Virginia, no other state weathered more Civil War battles than Tennessee. The struggle completely devastated the countryside. Large armies forged through cities, small towns, and rural communities. They took whatever they needed and destroyed what was left, depriving their enemies of resources.[4]

Regardless of their side in the Civil War, Tennesseans venerate Southern military leaders like Robert E. Lee, Thomas J. "Stonewall" Jackson, and Nathan Bedford Forrest. They view them the same way they think about men like President George Washington and Francis Marion, also known as the "Swamp Fox." Both were revered for their extraordinary exploits in the Revolutionary War. Marion, for example, was the first to use guerilla tactics and partisan warfare to defeat British General Charles Cornwallis in South Carolina. Marion learned these skills and tactics during the French and Indian Wars, applying them with renewed proficiency and hastening the war's end. Today, this type of warfare is referred to as "maneuver warfare," a concept employed by the United States Marine Corps as part of its official combat doctrine.[5] Marion's men served without pay throughout the war out of loyalty to him and firm belief in the righteousness of their cause.

Tennesseans hold Southern military leaders in high regard because of the confidence they inspire in the soldiers they lead. Washington took great care to ensure his soldiers could withstand the harsh winter at Valley Forge, Pennsylvania. He ordered his quartermaster to issue each soldier a daily rum staple and toured the encampment regularly, inspiring troops through his constant presence and genuine concern for their well-being. Nathan Bedford Forrest became legendary for his battle philosophy, "Be first with the most," a sentiment most Tennesseans saw as courage against all odds. Both sides of the Civil War respected Robert E. Lee and Stonewall Jackson for their unshakeable faith, leadership, and godly character.

Tennesseans often contrast men like Lee and Jackson against Union opponents like General William Tecumseh Sherman, who led his army on a scorched-earth campaign stretching from Atlanta, Georgia, to the shores of Savannah. Sherman gave his army free reign to terrorize civilians, pillage the countryside, and rape women. Revisionists try to justify the actions of Sherman and his men, reframing their efforts as "for the greater good of the Republic." But under a more biblical view, those who sow to the wind without repentance will most certainly reap the whirlwind of God's judgment (Job 4:8, Hosea 8:7). Sherman's actions were, clearly, crimes against humanity and a violation of the laws of war.[6]

Modern Southern Honor

During the First World War, the people of DeKalb County eagerly did their part. During the "War to End All Wars," ten of the county's residents were either killed in action or died of sickness. Sergeant Alvin C. York, a native of Fentress County, emerged as one of the war's most decorated soldiers. As a recipient of the Medal of Honor and the French Legion of Honor, York remains one of Tennessee's greatest heroes, ranking in status with people like David Crockett and President Andrew Jackson, better known as "Old Hickory."[7]

The Second World War was the most significant armed conflict in American history, and Tennesseans played an essential role in the Allied victory. Over 300,000 men from across the state served in America's armed forces, and six were decorated with the Congressional Medal of Honor, the nation's highest award for valor. In June 1941, DeKalb County hosted a series of military maneuvers featuring the combined forces of tanks and infantry. It was selected because the terrain was similar to that of Western Europe. There, General George S. Patton, who led the 2nd Armored Division and became one of America's greatest battle commanders, refined his innovative tactics for the aggressive use of tanks.

Throughout the war, hundreds of thousands of Tennesseans trained at places like Camp Campbell (known today as Fort Campbell) near Clarksville, Camp Forrest near Tullahoma, and Camp Tyson near Paris, Tennessee. These installations also housed thousands of Axis prisoners of war. Tennessee helped usher in the Atomic Age when Oak Ridge became one of the main sites for the top-secret Manhattan Project. The enriched uranium produced by Oak Ridge found its way into the atomic bombs dropped on Hiroshima and Nagasaki, which ended the war in the Pacific.[8]

Until the Second World War, women were forbidden to serve in the military, but that soon changed. Most women who volunteered for military service were kept on the sidelines, fulfilling mundane jobs.

Few of them faced combat or had the opportunity to serve overseas, but they were essential to the war effort behind the scenes. The women of DeKalb County eagerly embraced their duty, whether in the home or the service of their country. Several of them worked outside the home for the first time, taking jobs that supported the war machine. Some worked farms, while others organized fundraisers and blood drives for the American Red Cross. They willingly gave up the security and familiarity of home and family to contribute to winning the war.[9]

Postwar Boom

DeKalb County's economy centered on agriculture until the end of World War Two. In 1948, the U.S. Army Corps of Engineers completed the Center Hill Dam on the Caney Fork River, bringing hydroelectric power to the area. A garment factory soon opened, boosting the local economy and diversifying employment opportunities. Across the county, people began to find new, different sources of income in the war's aftermath.

Before going into business for herself, my mother worked at the Smithville Shirt Factory for over twenty years. The factory was built in the early 1950s and was poorly ventilated, making work challenging. Lint floated constantly through the air. The front door stayed open during the summer, with a large fan to help cool the facility. Unfortunately, most attempts at relief from the heat only intensified other problems—lint and dust. Mom enjoyed working there mainly for the social and economic benefits. She worked alongside neighbors and church members. Hers was the first generation to enjoy enough disposable income to purchase modern appliances such as stoves, refrigerators, and washing machines from local merchants.

My mother's philosophy was, "Where there's a will, there's a way." If you were willing, you could always find a way to rise above current circumstances. During the summer, when the heat and humidity were at their highest, she convinced several friends to wear bathing suits underneath their work clothes. That way, they could use their lunch break to enjoy a short picnic and swim at Evans Mill Dam, just a few miles away. Mom was a daring, rambunctious soul who believed rules were essential... but always subject to interpretation. People eagerly followed her, impressed by her courage and spontaneity.

A Young Boy's Paradise

The rural community of Blue Springs provided ample space for learning and adventure. It was a great place to develop a young boy's imagination, and it constantly challenged me to swim in deeper waters and reach beyond the familiar. Growing up on a small family farm, I learned a lot about how the world works. I became adept at problem-solving, as American farm boys are famous for doing. Through years of backbreaking work, I entered adulthood with a solid work ethic and an abundance of emotional and physical maturity. My school report card might have concealed it, but I had plenty of real-life experience and a solid, biblical foundation to become a stable, hardworking adult.

Before we were old enough to drive legally (we operated farm trucks long before we were of age), my older brother and I rode bicycles everywhere. Our parents were too busy to shuttle us around. Fortunately, Blue Springs was full of young people, providing a unique fellowship outside our immediate family. It was a close-knit community where young people spent a lot of time together, especially during the haying and tobacco-cutting seasons of summertime.

After a hard day's work on the farm, the older boys would take one of the trucks and head for the old country store, using the money they made that day to purchase bologna and crackers, canned pork and beans, a case of sodas (we called them "cold drinks"), and a handful of sweet Tennessee Crook cigars. Only a few boys had driver's licenses, but our employers didn't mind us using the trucks. They viewed it as a reward for a job well-done. We loaded the trucks and headed for our favorite swimming hole, where we built huge bonfires and skinny-dipped in the creek. Then, we would tell tall tales and fantasize about dating the prettiest girls in town. It was a carefree time that ticked away fast, considering the approaching storm of the Vietnam War and the 1960s counterculture.

Fred Cripps, my older brother and four years my senior, was always dutiful and seldom disappointed my parents. Whatever he set his mind to do, he always did it well—academics, sports, or social interaction. If there is such a thing as a born leader, Fred fit the bill. He was co-captain of the high school football team, helping to lead them to the regional playoffs in his senior year. Smithville held his graduating class, the Class of 1963, in high regard for their achievements on and off the field. They ventured into the world well-prepared, focused on making a name for themselves—and many did.

Our family had one rule for participating in high school extracurricular activities: you had to be home on time to help with the evening chores. In addition to their full-time jobs, our parents ran a small dairy farm. Dad stayed busy taking care of milking equipment, repairing tractors and machines, tending to the needs of the livestock, and checking fence lines for possible damage. We milked a combination of Jersey and Holstein cows, some of the most recognizable American breeds. Holsteins are large animals with beautiful color patterns, sometimes weighing eight hundred pounds or more.[10] Holsteins can be fussy and frustrating for one person to handle due to their size and temperament. Fred and I had to be on hand for the milking process, lending our muscles to keep it moving. We could not afford anyone to get hurt; it would have caused financial disaster.

Milking cows is a disciplined routine that requires preparation—much of it before daylight. Then, you must repeat the entire process in the evening. As the typical firstborn, Fred handled this responsibility well. He was reliable, driven, and self-motivated—all the qualities our parents appreciated and depended on to run the farm. Fred respected the demands our parents faced and worked hard to meet their expectations. He balanced the work requirements of the farm with his passion for other activities, like sports. Fred devised a simple plan that allowed him to engage in after-school events and still make it home to help Dad with evening chores. After football practice, Fred skipped socializing and went straight for the main highway, where he could hitch a ride home with afternoon traffic.

Clashing with Reality

After graduating from high school, Fred went to work in the natural gas industry in New Mexico. His departure left a vacuum in our little farming operation, which fell on my shoulders. My parents assumed I would approach the challenge by following in my brother's footsteps, but it was not to be. Unlike Fred, I was a daydreamer, preoccupied with internal reflections and lofty ideals that had little to do with the hard work of farming. It's incredible how you can grow up in the same house, under the same parents... and be so different.

I preferred to socialize and have fun. My favorite hangouts in those days were Webb's Drug Store, the Sunrise Grill, and Ernie's Restaurant. They've long since faded from the landscape, but they were havens for the young and the restless of the 1960s. After football practice during my first year, instead of heading straight home to help with the milking, I would arrange a rendezvous with my buddies at one of these places. I had no chance of getting home on time to help with chores.

After several days of getting home long past milking time, things came to a head with my parents. Dad was frustrated by my indifference. Mom was disenchanted with my failure to accept responsibility. I didn't fully understand it then, but they were calling me to my first shot at authentic, life-giving manhood—contributing to society and ensuring its future stability. I failed to appreciate the example Dad set for me. He courageously followed God's Word, loved and protected my mother, excelled at his work, and served the community's needs. Every man, with God's help, should aspire to this calling. Every woman longs for it, and every child deserves to see it modeled by their father.

I believe God makes the "first move" when someone needs intervention, and I needed it. It might happen through a stranger, an event or crisis, a friend or family member, or an unusual circumstance. God walks into our lives with a whisper (sometimes, a shout) and says, "I have a better way for you." I was the opposite of Fred: everything he did naturally, I did the reverse. But God hadn't forgotten me, nor was He content to let me remain the way I was. In hindsight, the growing discontent from my parents was the first "wake-up call" where I realized I could choose my response.

Plenty of things in life are beyond our control. Farm life teaches you to depend on things you can't control: weather, daylight, and cooperating with other people to succeed. But the work ethic I'd absorbed growing up on the farm was equally important. There are also many things about life that we *can* control. I was completely free to make wise decisions and prioritize my relationship with my family. Nobody could stop me from taking steps to reduce unnecessary stress and conflict. From that day forward, when I reached the halfway point of my journey home, I decided to jog the rest of the way to arrive home on time and avoid disappointing my parents.

The First Steps of the Long Run

My decision to jog seemed inconsequential at the time. But believe it or not, that's the secret of greatness—tiny, positive, seemingly insignificant changes in how we think, speak, or behave. It wouldn't have worked if I'd tried to change myself all at once and become like Fred. I couldn't fake enthusiasm for farming… but the more I jogged home, the better I became at running! Soon, I noticed I could run the entire way if I wanted. I discovered I could outrun my friends and fellow athletes in school, and I became a distance runner. When I entered military service, the daily requirement of running was easier for me than for most of my fellow soldiers. Decades later, I competed in the Marine Corps Marathon in Washington, DC.

If a minor conflict with my parents led me to make a small change… what kind of adaptations and character growth do you think are available in significant conflicts, like the battlefront of Vietnam?

Overseas combat helps warriors to develop perspective. It's a great "leveler" that equalizes everyone's footing. Enemy troops could care less if you come from a privileged background, hold a degree, or have a bright future back in your hometown. They don't care who your parents are or your family's reputation. They don't care about race, skin color, religion or gender. They'll pull the trigger all the same and never think twice about taking your life. Whatever you might have going for you back home, combat will show you how little it matters. You'll do way better in war if you're growing and improving on the *inside*—your spirit, soul, mind, and emotions.

Not everyone's insides are healthy, though. Combat and operational stress reactions, post-traumatic stress disorder (PTSD), and other emotional-related issues are just as indiscriminate as enemy troops. They don't respect anyone; they'll take you for everything you're worth. So, whether the battlefield is physical or in your mind… you'll discover just how little you truly control. That's the dilemma warriors face: we can't control others' behavior, or their decisions, or geopolitics, or enemy tactics. We can't even control the day of our own death. We can't go back and undo our past, and trying to forget it or pretend it doesn't exist is a mistake.

Yet as warriors, we carry the burdens of saving lives, preventing deaths, protecting civilians, and preserving our nation's way of life. We're issued weapons and trained for it. We're *supposed* to bring order and control and overcome impossible odds. We're *paid* to preserve a brighter future. How can we do that when so much is beyond our control?

If you lose sight of what you truly control, it's easy to go too far and become fatalistic—to believe that you have no power or influence over anything or anyone, so why bother? That's the very opposite of what this book is about and the attitudes that drive our terrible rates of depression, mental illness, alcoholism/drug abuse, homelessness, and suicide among veterans, not to mention our culture, which has completely lost sight of the concept of self-control.

I want to help you rediscover self-control and self-mastery because that's where your true power lies. The only thing we can really do, whether we clash with enemy troops or our own minds, is find the few things we genuinely control and change how we respond to what life throws at us—in the moment *and* for the future.

That is the true Hope of War.

Nestled in the heart of Middle Tennessee lies my hometown of Smithville. It is just an hour's drive from the bustling city of Nashville. Despite the proximity, Smithville remains a hidden gem that captures hearts year after year. The city is rich in history and has a unique, timeless vibe. Smithville's deeply-ingrained values and traditions create a warm and welcoming environment that makes visitors feel at home. As you wander the streets, you'll be captivated by the landscape, which transforms with every passing season. The vibrant hues of fall and the breathtaking spring are two examples of Smithville's natural charm that leave lasting impressions on visitors long after they've gone. Photo by Beth Chandler

Center Hill Lake is a stunningly beautiful lake in the heart of Middle Tennessee near my hometown of Smithville. The U.S. Army Corps of Engineers created the lake in 1948 by constructing a magnificent dam for electricity production and flood control. The serene waters of the lake and its captivating surroundings make it a popular destination for outdoor enthusiasts, nature lovers, and photographers. Photo adapted from public domain.

A family gathering on a Sunday afternoon in Dowelltown, TN, in the mid-1950s. The picture features my beloved parents, Freddie "Hoyte" Cripps (right) and Naomi "Sue" (Underwood) Cripps (center), along with my older brother, Fred, and me. We shared a deep love and strong bond as a family. Photos like this always fill me with nostalgia and precious memories.

My brother, Fred W. Cripps, was a responsible and dependable leader in high school. He served as a Navy Seabee with Naval Mobile Construction Battalion 121 during the Vietnam War. Later, he became the CEO of Distribution Construction Co. and was an authority in the natural gas industry. High school photo, 1963.

My father, Freddie "Hoyte" Cripps, was a brave young man who served his country during World War II. He joined the Navy and served aboard the USS Intrepid (CV-11), an Essex-class aircraft carrier of the Third Fleet, under Admiral William Frederick "Bull" Halsey Jr. The USS Intrepid played a vital role in the fleet, participating in many battles and operations in the Pacific Theater of the war. Dad earned a Bronze Star Medal, Combat Action Ribbon, and five bronze campaign stars for his service in the Pacific Theater. He was proud to serve and contribute to the war effort, but he never talked about it unless he was with other veterans.

Chapter Two
The Would-Be Lions

**"Heroes are made from raw courage, circumstances with few options, and situations that demand a response.
In warfare, when an enemy blows your boat out of the water, you have three choices—surrender, sink, or swim.
Swimming is always more demanding."[1]**

"I am not afraid of an army of lions led by a sheep, but I do fear an army of sheep led by a lion."[2]
- Alexander the Great

"What lives in the darkness, dies in the light."
- Pastor Jack Hayford

Finding hope in war takes courage, and "courage" has several meanings.

I have tremendous respect for everyone who wears the military uniform. But some warriors go through their entire lives and careers without facing their biggest archenemy: themselves. Everyone has to reckon with their own dark side—laziness, anger, selfishness, self-pity, hatred, pride, or self-righteousness. Until you learn to deal with how your "lower" self shows up, you're a double-minded person.

When you're misaligned, you compromise your values and integrity. You sabotage yourself, and in the process, you sabotage others who depend on you. It undermines your level of courage. This will come back to haunt you when you least expect it.

You've probably heard the definition of integrity if you've served in the military: "Do what the situation requires, regardless of who is looking." I would add, "regardless of the outcome." Sometimes, exercising courage and integrity isn't a win-win. Occasionally, one person must make a sacrifice so that others win—but they themselves get left behind. Think of the classic example of one soldier falling on a live grenade so his battle buddies can escape. Sometimes, we must risk, or even lose, our lives to find them.

As I learned the meaning of courage, I thought of Dietrich Bonhoeffer. He was a German Lutheran pastor, theologian, anti-Nazi dissident, and a founding member of the Confessing Church. During the early days of the Nazi regime, Bonhoeffer trained young clergy illegally at a Confessing Church seminary in Finkenwalde, which the Gestapo closed in September 1937. He spent the next two years traveling throughout eastern Germany to supervise his students, most of whom shepherded secret, small parishes. Eventually, the Nazis banned Bonhoeffer from Berlin altogether. In 1940, they issued an order forbidding him to speak publicly; Bonhoeffer ignored it.

The first deportations of Berlin Jews began on October 15, 1941. A few days later, Bonhoeffer and Friedrich Perels, a Confessing Church lawyer, wrote a letter describing the deportations to trusted German military officials, hoping it might move them to some corrective action. Bonhoeffer became peripherally involved in "Operation Seven," a plan to help Jews escape from Germany by giving them official documentation as foreign agents. After the Nazis discovered the plan, they arrested Bonhoeffer and his brother-in-law, Hans von Dohnanyi, in April 1943. Bonhoeffer's connections to the broader resistance came to light after a failed coup attempt against Adolf Hitler on July 20, 1944, and the Nazis moved him to a Gestapo prison in Berlin. On April 9, 1945, as the regime collapsed, they hanged Bonhoeffer.

Shortly before he ascended the gallows, he wrote, "The ultimate test of a moral society is the kind of world it leaves to its children." But I would add that the ultimate test of those children is what they do with the world left to them by their parents.

The World We Received

The Baby Boom Generation, born and raised in the aftermath of the Second World War (1946 to 1964), received an idyllic, prosperous, and peaceful world from our parents. The German and Japanese war machines were smashed and defeated. The United States lost half a million men to World War II, but we emerged victorious as the world's lone (and only nuclear-armed) superpower. Technology and life expectancy improved dramatically in the 1950s. Inflation was low, life was affordable, and the middle class swelled in numbers. Faith, patriotism, and stability formed the foundations of the cultural climate.

But for the most part, we Boomers failed to appreciate it. Growing up, we claimed we had more wisdom than our forebears. We rejected traditional American values as "too old-fashioned" for the times. As we entered the 1960s, we carved out a new future based on *individualism*—the idea that what we believe and how we live is inconsequential to anyone but ourselves. Along with our perspectives, we changed our appearance, attire, and how we related to authority figures. We adopted words like "love," "peace," and "freedom" as slogans without truly understanding their meaning. We bragged about being the largest, most educated, and most influential generation in American history. We believed we had the power to change America's political, economic, and social landscape and liberate the country from the suffocating sensibilities of our parents.

During the ensuing upheaval, our perception of "truth" shifted far to the left of our parents. We cast aside customary moral boundaries and became indifferent, callous, and cynical. We boasted of knowing the price of everything… but truthfully, we knew the value of nothing.

We embarked on quests for new pleasures and experiences. These became the "drugs" we needed to numb the pain of our empty, meaningless existence. Where there is a lack of moral leadership, each generation must decide how to confront the world—either change it or be changed by it.[3] Sadly, we only *thought* we'd chosen the former; in fact, we chose the latter.

Established American institutions, like family, religion, education, and government, buckled down as we began questioning them. The music of the times served as a vehicle for social change. Imagine yourself amid a kaleidoscope, surrounded by an explosion of colors and patterns that continuously shift, evolve, and intertwine—that's what it felt like. In the 1960s, we pushed boundaries. New fields of music emerged, and the power of art, song, and film changed society forever. You may not have experienced this era firsthand, but if you look closely, you can feel its impact rippling into today's themes and culture.[4]

Artists like Bob Dylan and Joan Baez broke away from traditional music styles and focused on expressions of raw emotion through their songs. They condemned the wealthy, America's justice system, the Cold War, and race-related violence. This newfound free expression resonated with young audiences disillusioned with the day's political turmoil and societal constraints. Dylan's songs "Blowin' in the Wind" and "The Times They Are a-Changin,'"[5] challenged societal norms, stirred up listeners, and shook society to its core.

Dance crazes swept across the nation as young people eagerly embraced new, liberating and energetic music. Vinyl records by bands like The Beatles, The Rolling Stones, and The Who flew off the shelves. The frenzy also impacted fashion and style, changing how people expressed themselves through clothing and personal appearance. The music of the Sixties catalyzed social change everywhere—civil rights, war, racial and gender equality, and peace.

Moral Compromise Meets Another Reckoning

Closer to home, outrage erupted on February 1, 1960, when 17-year-old Franklin McCain and three black friends took a seat at the whites-only lunch counter at a Woolworth's department store in Greensboro, North Carolina. It triggered a movement that propelled the nation from its segregated past to a more inclusive future. By the time I entered high school in the fall of 1963, the evening news was dominated by scenes of civil rights protesters battling segregationists and entrenched authorities in the South.

Malcolm Little, better known as "Malcolm X," rose to prominence during the early days of the civil rights movement. He was an American Muslim minister and civil rights activist. Reflecting on the Greensboro legacy, he said, "In three difficult years, the southern struggle has grown from a modest group of black students to the largest mass movement for racial reform and civil rights in the 20th century."[6] But the pace and trajectory of racial reform weren't limited to the United States; they were global. Two days after the McCain incident in Greensboro, British Prime Minister Harold MacMillan addressed South Africa's parliament in Cape Town with a warning: "The wind of change is blowing through this continent," he said. "Whether we like it or not, this growth of national consciousness is a political fact."[7]

Greensboro was the beginning of a long road that eventually led to a worldwide movement for racial reform. On August 28, 1963, Dr. Martin Luther King, Jr. delivered his famous "I Have a Dream" speech at the March on Washington, D.C., for Jobs and Freedom. The rally drew some 250,000 people, roughly a quarter of whom were white. This was the beginning of the end for segregation laws, along with the graphic scenes of police officers in Birmingham, Alabama, using dogs and high-pressure water hoses on blacks, including children as young as six.[8]

More Compromises with Darkness

Meanwhile, the U.S. military presence slowly expanded in South Vietnam. At first, our role was strictly advisory; Southeast Asia hardly ever made the evening news. However, the U.S. figured prominently as a negotiator in the Geneva Treaty of 1954, where colonial France withdrew from Indochina. In a fragile settlement with the communist powers of Russia and China, the Western powers agreed to divide Vietnam into a communist north and a free south, setting the stage for future conflict.

The Cold War in Europe and in Cuba, where the regime of Fidel Castro had seized power, dominated the headlines in the early Sixties. After the disastrous Bay of Pigs invasion and the Cuban Missile Crisis, President John F. Kennedy delivered his famous "Ich bin ein Berliner" speech in West Berlin on June 26, 1963. The Soviet Union had already shot down the American U-2 spy plane and erected the Berlin Wall to prevent mass German emigration to West Berlin. Western fears of communist aggression and expansionism reached a fever pitch.

Kennedy's speech was as much a warning to the Soviets as it was a message of solidarity with captive East Berliners. He made clear the United States would continue to support West Germany, whatever the Soviets did, and faithfully resist communist expansionism.[9] To that end, he reasoned, the U.S. was responsible to counter Moscow's meddling in Vietnam, which persisted after they gained independence from France.

Unfortunately, the "Ich bin ein Berliner" speech was Kennedy's last appearance on the world stage. Three months later, on November 22, 1963, Lee Harvey Oswald assassinated Kennedy in Dallas, Texas. The Viet Cong, however, continued to grow stronger with Soviet funding and supplies.

Crumbling (and Rising) Hope

I was leaving the high school gym when the news broke that Kennedy had been shot while riding in an open-car motorcade. In the following hours, people across the globe gathered around television sets for reports. Many wondered whether there was a larger, more sinister plot against the United States. There was a concern for the safety of Vice President Lyndon B. Johnson, who rode two cars behind Kennedy in the motorcade. The news shocked the entire nation, and many wept as the reports spread. The Kennedy assassination had a worldwide ripple effect, much like the Japanese attack on Pearl Harbor on December 7, 1941, and the September 11, 2001, terrorist attacks.[10]

Worldwide mourning over President Kennedy's death exceeded the typical grief over the loss of a national leader. Many considered Kennedy the last hope for peace against Soviet expansionism. His election kindled the hopes and dreams of young and old alike. But his untimely death deprived America and the world of his optimism, innovation, and stirring imagination.

Domestically, Kennedy had sought to remedy pockets of need that he identified by race, region, and age, focusing mainly on the nation's poorest citizens. More boldly, he made it a national priority to land Americans on the moon by the decade's end.

Some aspects of Kennedy's legacy invoke fond memories, while others don't. People preferred the mystique over the man. Only later did we learn of his severe back problems, which required steady doses of potent medications for him to function. Privately, he had a voracious sexual appetite, and he became infamous for his indiscretions. Kennedy's decisions bungled the Bay of Pigs invasion, which set the stage for the Cuban Missile Crisis and accelerated the spread of communism around the world, including Vietnam.

Congressional conservatives dissuaded Kennedy from acting on proposed civil rights legislation, only for popular groundswells like the Civil Rights Movement to rise and force his hand.[11] Despite his flaws and limited experience in foreign policy, I believe God used Kennedy's inspirational leadership to spur the country into action to address the needs of neighbors at home and in the forgotten corners of the world.

Shortly before the assassination, Bob Dylan released his song, "The Times They Are A-Changin'." It speculated that something was about to happen that would change everything. Dylan's prophecy was eerily accurate; a decade of cultural revolution ensued. The long-range impact of these transformations echoes through to the present day, reminding us how far we've drifted from our traditional moral and spiritual moorings.

But another wave of change still approached. Dylan never saw it coming. I doubt he recognized it when it arrived or recognizes it today. I don't know if he ever will.

This kind of revolution went much deeper than clothing, hair length, music, or slogans. It's the kind of change only God can bring about, through the journey of a warrior's *maturity*. It takes place far away from the lights and cameras of media coverage, in the hearts and souls of the men and women who offer their lives in service on the battlefield. It's a change that leads to lasting joy, permanent hope, and abundant life.

I doubt most of my generation found this path during the empty pursuits of the Sixties. Even many of the men who served didn't find it. But I did... and I wasn't the only one. With hindsight, I can see the beginnings of a much more meaningful revolution... beginning in the small town of Smithville, Tennessee, before I even left for war.

Choose Your Revolution

Most people's high school experiences set the foundations for their adulthood. That's certainly how it went for me. Dr. James Dobson, one of America's most respected Christian counselors, says the decisions we make between the ages of sixteen and twenty-six form the principles and values that govern our lives. The impact of mistakes and bad choices during this period lasts, in some cases, for decades. As when a bricklayer fails to get his foundation straight, we suddenly wield the power to undermine significant parts of our future, through decisions made on a whim. Young people need great mentors during these critical years.[12]

My academic performance throughout high school was marginal at best, despite others' expectations. If we measure ourselves using someone else's yardstick, I stood for measurement against my older brother, Fred. His popularity and achievements were hard to rival, so I aimed at a different target. In my search for significance, I leaned my ladder against all the walls he avoided. Hungry for recognition, I "worked hard" at being reckless and rebellious. I became an expert at pushing the envelope, venturing beyond limits and into treacherous waters. (But stick with me—not everything about daredevils is bad!)

Once, while scaling the lofty bluffs overlooking Center Hill Lake near downtown Smithville, an enormous boulder broke loose underneath my feet. I plunged some fifty feet into the water below, and the boulder almost landed on top of me. It was a stark reminder that anything can happen when you continuously live that close to the edge. But did I think of my narrow escape that way? Not at all! In my mind, the adrenaline rush of the moment far outweighed the risks. If foolishness is the misuse of godly intelligence, my teenage years made me a poster boy for it. I lived in my own fantasy world, believing what happened to others would never happen to me.

But there are no shortcuts to becoming a true lion—a leader others want to follow, whose boldness compels them to keep pushing forward, come hell or high water. If you've seen action in combat, you know that "hell" shows up. (And high water, too—especially in the rainy season in Vietnam.) The recklessness of a teenage boy is not the same as the boldness of a lion. Serving alongside my combat brothers in Vietnam transformed me from the former to the latter. God used the war to dispose of my presumptuous, self-assured heart and embrace the meaning of the biblical proverb, "The fear of the Lord is the beginning of wisdom" (Proverbs 9:10). Most young people in America in the Sixties chose one type of revolution; I simply chose another.

As I said, daredevils have some good qualities. Risking my life in Vietnam proved it because sometimes, the way of the lion is the opposite of what you might think. The path looks reckless and doomed to fail, and everything in you tells you to turn around and run away. Instead, you must deliberately expose yourself to danger. It "looks" like you're playing roulette and allowing the enemy to train his scope on you while he takes his best shot. Plenty of missions in Vietnam, intentionally or not, involved just that—we waited for the enemy to take the bait and take a shot at us. Sometimes, we *knew* they'd laid a trap for us, and we provoked them deliberately.

Sometimes, being a lion means you *take* the hit. Jesus, whom the Book of Revelation calls "the Lion of Judah," never shied away from revealing Himself and taking hits from the Pharisees and Romans. Neither did Bonhoeffer; he knew the risks of publicly challenging Adolf Hitler and his henchmen—and he did it anyway. After he was arrested and imprisoned, he continued to live out his faith and serve his fellow prisoners. Even as he approached the gallows in Flossenburg Concentration Camp, Bonhoeffer spoke against evil. He goaded the enemy at every turn, daring them to take their best shot. I went through a few moments like that, too.

But how do you know, from one moment to the next, which kind of situation you're dealing with? Do you quietly spring the trap, forcing the enemy out into the open to fight him? Or do you reveal your position with a yell, let the enemy retaliate, and risk that your number might be next? That's a tough one. I believe it's why God gives us His Spirit; most of the time, we don't pay enough attention to notice.

A Time for Grieving Bad Choices

On any given day, you and I might avoid the price that men like Jesus and Dietrich Bonhoeffer paid for making themselves vulnerable. I escaped numerous "spring the trap" missions in Vietnam. But everyone will pay a price for failing to battle the darkness within. That's the only choice that leads to certain death.

Long after Vietnam ended, I learned a more important lesson: I had to battle my inner darkness by grieving the innocence I lost there and purging the guilt I felt for surviving. In some ways, I matured by serving in combat. In other ways, I altogether avoided maturity well into middle-age. I hid from my own worst enemy: myself.

Even today, if you serve in uniform, you must understand—you can't keep your guard up and wear your armor constantly, never letting other people in. Eventually, the truth will force itself to the surface. What will you do then? Where could Nazi collaborators and sympathizers hide when the Allies reduced the Third Reich to rubble? What excuse did average Germans have when Allied soldiers discovered the gas chambers and ovens of Nazi concentration camps? The darkness we entertain will come back to haunt us somehow.

What will *you* do when your sorrow, guilt, shame, and anger surface and your dark side is exposed? What have you done with these emotions when they appeared? Have you become angry? Violent? Have you turned to drugs and alcohol, illicit affairs, or workaholism? Have you tried to run away and hide from the truth?

The truth is usually the "underdog" in the battle for your soul. It's a minority voice because you're working overtime against a stronger, louder, more visceral enemy.

In the Bible, when King David faced Goliath, everyone watching predicted David would get torn to pieces. Goliath was a giant, a trained warrior, a fully-grown adult—and he terrified the entire Israelite army. David was a teenage shepherd boy, despised by his brothers (who all served in the Israelite army) and who declined to wear the king's armor. David didn't exist merely in the minority... he *was* the minority! Of the whole Israelite camp, David alone believed Goliath could be defeated. Imagine being on a battlefield with two entire armies—tens of thousands of adult soldiers on *both* sides—who think your opponent has a one hundred percent chance of winning!

David didn't listen to any of the voices telling him to be afraid or run away. He listened to the one voice he'd learned to trust as a shepherd: the voice of God. David understood something profound: victory doesn't *always* go to the bigger, stronger, or more numerous combatants—especially if you fight as a child of God.

Does any of that describe how you feel? Are you overwhelmed by loud voices of guilt, sorrow, and regret? Does your military service, past or present, feel meaningless or like a waste of time? Do you hear a thousand voices lamenting loss and despair, like David did? If so, you might need to make a change—perhaps a small one, like the decision to run home I mentioned in the last chapter. Or you might need to walk out on the ledge, remove your armor, and let somebody help you.

The Lion's Underbelly

The pain you feel, the unresolved issues… could they be pointing toward something you've been unwilling to see? Could you find true freedom right under your nose in the very place you've come to think of as a prison? If so, do you really want to miss out on it?

Many warriors think *lionheartedness* means "dominance, strength, and aggression." They picture someone fearlessly moving against enemy troops, resisting interrogation with an iron will, and winning the battle of the day. They picture a modern-day knight slaying the dragon and winning the lady's heart. Those are great attributes, but the picture is incomplete.

It's incomplete because no great warrior's heart is divided against itself through compromise. Most of the cowardice, capitulation, and surrender we associate with modern wars, beginning with Vietnam, can be traced to the moral failures and spiritual unease we've taken on before and since the Sixties. We've made too much room for darkness in our own souls. It went so viral among my generation that we elevated it to the level of a righteous cause: the "counterculture."

As a result, many Vietnam veterans fail, to this day, to see the merit in what we did. Our veterans are compromised by the way they've made room for darkness. If there's one thing worse than being compromised, it's the terror we feel at exposing our failure to the light by confessing it. The last thing we want others to know is that we're afraid, wracked with guilt, some aspect of our lives has spun out of control, or that we were so blinded that we never stopped to think or look from a different perspective. Instead, we hide the ugly parts, often behind bravado or machismo.

Maybe it's time to drop the façade. Perhaps you've got some deeper digging to do.

You'll need help from people qualified enough to speak into your situation, who care enough to listen and can see things about you that you don't see yourself. But if you're going to find the Hope of War, you must make room for your own humanity.

You can't shed weaknesses just by putting on a uniform.

The weaknesses will still plague you, no matter what clothes you wear.

And unless you deal with those weaknesses head-on, they will follow you for the rest of your life.

Remember the lesson from Chapter One: *make one small change*. Instead of bottling up your frustration, resentment, cynicism, or whatever negative emotion you feel concerning the service and sacrifice you made, find someone you trust and get it off your chest. Let them know you simply need a sounding board. Get it out of your system and into the light, where the Spirit of God can help you process it.

When you're finished, don't be surprised if you feel a little more hopeful. This is a huge part of the Hope of War.

Chapter Three
Standing Your Ground When the Storm Approaches

War is a breeding ground for deceit, injustice, and misguided ambitions used to distract those who seek truth.
Truth is the only sure path to freedom…
which is why the mighty tremble in its presence.[1]

Once you understand how deeply courage and vulnerability are intertwined, you might begin to see why the world is filled with so much deceit, inequity, and misguided ambitions. Everybody desires to project strength, skill, and resilience, but few want to take the risk of being honest about their dark side. It's not easy confronting our own motives because they often expose our inadequacy. So instead, we hide.

This "hiding" tendency leaves few people genuinely qualified to carry the mantle of leadership. If you look closely, it's a core human issue most of us never escape. As water molecules "attract" one another, forming a puddle, so the "great mass of men lead lives of quiet desperation," as Henry David Thoreau said, and they attract one another until they form something worse, like an angry mob.

Yearning for significance and terrified of being exposed for their inadequacy, my generation took to the streets to point fingers at anyone and anything they could credibly accuse. This is one of the Baby Boomers' ugliest legacies. It never works… not even if you make it as far as the Oval Office. To be clear, I believe there was plenty of treachery and deceit in the buildup to the Vietnam War. But the older I get, the more clearly I see how my fellow Boomers used the war to distract from their own emptiness.

My generation failed to engage and fulfill their calling. Those of us who chose to go to Vietnam weren't "better" than those who avoided it. But by going, we went through a masterclass in leadership, which our contemporaries forfeited. We learned enduring lessons from conflict and struggle. We learned to embrace responsibility, and we discovered the deeper meaning of concepts like duty, honor, and abiding faith. We acquired a perspective our peers never would and tremendous potential for wielding a positive influence on people. Over 27 million men were eligible for service in Vietnam, but less than half of them answered the call. If you have ears to hear it, today—I believe we who answered acquired the physical and spiritual scars of the vulnerable side of lionheartedness. Our contemporaries ... simply didn't.

Of all the things I treasure from my days in the jungle, the ability to handle horrible circumstances and confront my own inner darkness with honor, dignity, and humanity is the most precious. Though it took me a long time, I found peace, breakthrough, and redemption—and then I set about spreading it to my fellow warriors. The most powerful gift I can give you through the pages of this book is the skill to embrace this "double-sided" version of courage—strength *and* vulnerability. Only with both can we genuinely stand our ground when storms approach.

Sir Winston Churchill, British statesman and former Prime Minister of the United Kingdom, once said, "To each, there comes in their lifetime a special moment when they are figuratively tapped on the shoulder and offered the chance to do an extraordinary thing, unique to them and fitted to their talents. What a tragedy if that moment finds them unprepared or unqualified for what could have been their finest hour."[2]

I'm saddened that so many of my generation passed up their opportunity. When they could have stood their ground, they fled, told lies, levied accusations, or made bargains and excuses. They did just about anything *except* answer the call.

But to be fair, they didn't exactly have the finest leaders to follow.

LBJ: The Tarnished Legacy

After John F. Kennedy's death, Lyndon Johnson ascended to the presidency with enormous political capital. He spearheaded several sweeping legislative reforms, using his congressional experience to accelerate them, and won reelection in a landslide the following year. Building on Kennedy's foundation, President Johnson set about transforming America into a "Great Society" that eradicated poverty and racial injustice.[3] Working around the clock, he persuaded former colleagues in both houses of Congress to support legislation that would ensure the less fortunate had a "hand up, rather than a handout."

Some of Johnson's new initiatives included Medicare and Medicaid, social programs designed to help elderly and low-income people pay for costly medical care. He initiated the National Head Start program to help meet the emotional, social, nutritional, and psychological needs of preschool-aged children from low-income families. Johnson instituted the Job Corps under the administration of the U.S. Department of Labor. This program's mission was to help young people, ages sixteen through twenty-four, improve their quality of life through vocational and academic training.

By far, the biggest milestone of Johnson's first year as president was the Civil Rights Act of 1964, which ended racial segregation.[4] The law had a cascading effect, setting in motion several other reforms, such as equal housing legislation and the Voting Rights Act, the following year. The VRA dismantled legal barriers at state and local levels designed to prevent African Americans from exercising their right to vote under the 15th Amendment to the U.S. Constitution.[5]

Personally, Johnson was familiar with the poverty and hardship he sought to eradicate. Despite being the son of a member of the Texas legislature (Sam Ealy Johnson, Jr.), he didn't come from a wealthy family. Johnson worked throughout his childhood and youth in rural Texas, where modern conveniences like electricity had not yet spread. His father suffered massive financial setbacks, from which his family never recovered. All of this gave him a deep sense of compassion for people living in poverty.

In early adulthood, Johnson found his way into politics as a congressional aide. He met and married Claudia A. Taylor, nicknamed "Lady Bird," in 1934. When Johnson decided to run for Congress in Austin's 10th District, Lady Bird supported her husband's political ambitions using inheritance money from her mother's estate to finance his campaign.[6] Lady Bird was a highly accomplished woman with an excellent head for business. She owned radio and television stations in Austin, and she was a millionaire in her own right. Johnson repaid her devotion by engaging, among other things, in numerous extramarital affairs. But he won the election to the U.S. House of Representatives in 1937. For the next three decades, Johnson enjoyed a political career where he won nearly every race he undertook. He finished the journey in the White House—the highest office of them all.

When Japan attacked Pearl Harbor in December 1941, drawing the U.S. into World War Two, Johnson enlisted in the Naval Reserve. If he assumed military service would enhance his political prospects… he was correct. In mid-1942, wearing the rank of lieutenant commander, Johnson traveled to the Southwest Pacific Theater as an observer. There he reported to General Douglas MacArthur, who gave permission for him to sit in on an aerial bombing raid against Japanese targets. At an airstrip in Port Moresby, New Guinea, Johnson boarded a B-26 Marauder, dubbed the *Wabash Cannonball.* Shortly before takeoff, Johnson found his seat occupied by another officer, forcing him to hitch a ride on a separate B-26, the *Heckling Hare.* As it turned out, the *Wabash Cannonball* was shot down later that day, killing everyone on board.

As he recounted, years after the loss of the *Wabash Cannonball,* Johnson's plane came under attack from several Japanese Zeros, forcing the crew to abort its bombing mission altogether. The pilot, Lieutenant Walter Greer, struggled to evade the Zeros as the crew operated the guns to keep them at bay. It took several minutes for

Greer to shake his pursuers, and they returned to Moresby with only one engine. It was the kind of drama from which movies are made.

Though Johnson himself played no active part in the mission, MacArthur awarded him the Silver Star—the third-highest U.S. combat medal for bravery—for his apparent "coolness" under fire. The other crew members—including Lieutenant Greer, whose flying skill saved Johnson's life—received no medal of any kind. Greer wasn't even aware of Johnson's Silver Star until he read about it in the newspaper. Meanwhile, the men who died on the *Wabash Cannonball* only received a lower-ranking Purple Heart for their part in the mission.[7] In a scene familiar to many veterans, the real heroes received menial recognition, while the politicians leapt to claim the credit.

It seems Vietnam was not the first war to entertain dishonesty, nor was it the first to produce future political leaders with little regard for the truth. Initially, Johnson showed embarrassment about being labeled a hero. He told a Washington reporter he didn't deserve the medal and submitted a letter to its originator asking for it to be rescinded. But in the end, he accepted the award, wore the lapel pin with pride, and referred to it often on the campaign trail throughout his political career.

Years later, surviving crew members revealed that the *Heckling Hare* never reached its target due to mechanical problems. The plane was never at risk from Japanese fighters. Johnson's biographer, Robert Dallek, said the Silver Star resulted from a deal with General MacArthur in return for Johnson's solemn pledge, as a member of Congress, to lobby President Franklin Roosevelt for more war supplies in the Southwest Pacific Theater.[8] It was a textbook example of the dark side of culture and politics—a leader using the "opportunities" of crisis and war to feed his personal ambitions.

Rising to Power

Back home, Johnson became a master politician who used his influence to persuade opponents in Congress. He was known for "strong-arming" them into seeing things his way. According to a pair of *New York Times* journalists of the day, Johnson developed a reputation for giving people "The Treatment":

> *"The Treatment" could last ten minutes or four hours. It came, enveloping its target, at the Johnson Ranch swimming pool, in one of Johnson's offices, in the Senate cloakroom, on the floor of the Senate itself—wherever Johnson might find a fellow senator within his reach. Its tone could be supplication, accusation, cajolery, exuberance, scorn, tears, complaint, and the hint of threat. It was all of these together. It ran the gamut of human emotions. Its velocity was breathtaking and it was all in one direction. Interjections from the target were rare. Johnson anticipated them before they could be spoken. He moved in close, his face a scant millimeter from his target, his eyes widening and narrowing, his eyebrows rising and falling. From his pockets poured clippings, memos, statistics. Mimicry, humor, and the genius of analogy made "The Treatment" an almost hypnotic experience and rendered the target stunned and helpless.*

Johnson served throughout the 1940s in the House of Representatives and spent the 1950s in the U.S. Senate. He served two terms as Senate Minority Leader, another two as Senate Majority Whip, and six years as Senate Majority Leader. Johnson understood the inner workings of Washington better than most and knew where all the right pressure points lay.[9] He is regarded by the Senate today as its most effective majority leader in history, because of his legendary ability to gather detailed intelligence on the positions and priorities of every senator with whom he served.

Although Johnson's legislative initiatives had a lasting impact on the nation, his decision to commit U.S. military ground forces to Southeast Asia overshadowed them. It forced his administration to redirect funds from the War on Poverty to the War in Vietnam, which consumed most of his administration's time and focus.

When Strength and Intimidation Stop Working

The 1964 presidential election took place one year after Kennedy's assassination. During the campaign, Johnson presented himself as a "peace candidate," promising not to widen America's military involvement in Vietnam. At one Ohio press conference, he said he had "no intentions of sending American boys to some distant land to do what Asian boys ought to be doing for themselves."[10] But after his victory over Senator Barry Goldwater, Johnson immediately reassessed the possibility of military intervention in Vietnam. As a cautionary measure, he announced an increase in military conscriptions, from 17,000 to 35,000 per month.[11]

Until the middle of 1964, the total number of U.S. military advisors in South Vietnam stood at 16,000. Then, in August, a clash between U.S. Naval forces and North Vietnamese patrol boats in the Gulf of Tonkin marked an escalation in the Cold War struggle for Southeast Asia. Johnson authorized retaliatory air strikes against Hanoi naval bases and spiked U.S. military involvement in defense of South Vietnam.[12]

Johnson believed America's ally, South Vietnam, was losing the fight against the Viet Cong communist guerrillas. In a conversation with his staff, Johnson said he did not want to be known as "the president who allowed Southeast Asia to fall to the communists," as had happened to President Harry Truman with China in 1949.[13] Johnson believed the assault would force communist North Vietnam to stop providing military support to the Viet Cong. Ultimately, the bombing of Hanoi did little to stave off the flow of supplies down the Ho Chi Minh Trail–a network of bicycle trails, hastily-built dirt roads, and meandering footpaths from North Vietnam, through the neutral border countries of Cambodia and Laos, and into South Vietnam.[14]

Johnson then persuaded Congress to pass the Gulf of Tonkin Resolution, which gave him broad authority to do whatever he felt necessary to protect American interests in Vietnam.[15] The demand for troops mushroomed, making it impossible for annual benchmark enlistments to keep pace with the ever-growing demands, so Johnson ordered an expansion of the draft. Over the next four years, the Selective Service would conscript, on average, some 300,000 young men into service every year.[16]

How Would You Handle It?

For a moment, imagine you were President Johnson at this pivotal moment in history. How would you think about yourself?

You overcame poverty and deprivation and found a winning career track as a politician. You served in World War Two and received a Silver Star from America's most beloved military leader. You served twelve years in Congress and held three distinguished leadership positions, where you built up a tremendous record of legislative accomplishments. You served as vice president under one of the nation's most beloved presidents. You ascended, unelected, to the highest office in the land and became the leader of the free world. Once sworn in, you spearheaded numerous sweeping reforms that reshaped American culture at breakneck speed, and you got elected to your first full term as president in a 44-state landslide. Going forward, you had the opportunity to be re-elected to a second term in 1968 and become the longest-serving president since Franklin Roosevelt. You retaliated against communist aggression in Southeast Asia, and Congress granted you broad power to crush the North Vietnamese enemy.

Would you feel like a lion? Maybe like the king of the castle?

According to another Johnson biographer, Robert Caro, Johnson's true ambition was to be remembered as a genuine social reformer in the image of President Roosevelt. Few political figures leave an enduring legacy the way Roosevelt did. Elected during the Great Depression, FDR ushered in enormous reforms and guided his country through World War Two, one of the darkest times in American history. Johnson often eulogized FDR as his most admired political hero, claiming he found inspiration for his own "Great Society" legislation from FDR's "New Deal" legacy.[17]

With these new powers from the Gulf of Tonkin Resolution, perhaps Johnson could become both a social reformer and a beloved wartime leader, just like Roosevelt. It was as close as he would ever get to fulfilling that final dream of continuing in the tradition of Roosevelt.

But remember—there's more to being lionhearted than advancing forcefully, crushing your enemies, and dividing the spoils of prosperity. Battlefield dominance and material wealth are no substitute for truth and character.

Lingering Inadequacy

At first, Johnson felt "illegitimate"—a pretender on the throne without any authentic presidential covering. His lack of self-confidence surfaced quickly. He was reluctant to trust the people around him, including the Joint Chiefs of Staff, the National Security Council or the Secretary of Defense. Johnson's quest for reassurance and support, rather than a wide-range debate on policy issues, colored his relationships and determined America's foreign policy more than anything else, particularly in Vietnam.[18]

As the military prepared for large-scale deployments of air and ground combat units, Johnson encountered political pressure from Defense Secretary Robert McNamara and the Joint Chiefs of Staff. They wanted him to petition Congress to call up the military's National Guard and Reserve units. Johnson later wrote in his memoirs that he didn't want to "make a threatening scene to the Chinese or the Russians by calling up the reserves in large numbers." In truth, Johnson was presented with a political problem: he didn't want to face the ire of wealthy, influential supporters, many of whom were legislators or campaign contributors. Their sons had joined the National Guard or Reserves to avoid the draft–and the parents didn't want them activated for service in Vietnam.[19]

By deferring to those supporters, Johnson bucked nearly two hundred years of precedent. In every war since the American Revolution, the Militia—the predecessor of the National Guard and Reserve—joined the fight. Kennedy mobilized them for the Berlin Wall and the Cuban Missile Crises of 1961-62. The Guard and Reserve, already smarting under reputations as havens for draft dodgers, disagreed with the president's policy and expressed their desire to participate. But Johnson firmly refused to activate them.

Once you tell the first lie, the next one becomes easier to tell. It turned out that the casual dishonesty Johnson developed from actions like accepting the Silver Star in exchange for political favors had consequences. As much as he'd achieved, his credibility was compromised—before a single pair of American boots hit the ground in the jungles of Vietnam. Now, Johnson was "picking and choosing" who he sent to war based on superficial characteristics and his own political interests… and people noticed.

In contrast, the Second World War drafted *everyone* capable of serving between the ages of eighteen and forty-five. Since the war's end, young men between eighteen and twenty-five have been required to register with the Selective Service in case of a national emergency. However, beginning with the Korean Conflict in the 1950s, the government granted "deferments" to college students, allowing them to postpone military service until they completed their education. This controversial new policy allowed wealthier students to avoid the draft.[20] One criticism of the Vietnam War was how it placed the burden of fighting on the backs of working-class and low-income American youth (fifty-five percent and twenty-five percent, respectively).[21] In Vietnam, soldiers often joked, "Where are the sons of all the big shots who supported this war? They're certainly not in my platoon!"

Johnson's increased draft calls created a chain reaction among young American men. Although only twenty-five percent of the warriors who served in Vietnam between 1965 and 1975 were draftees, conscription motivated many to "volunteer" for military service, hoping to get occupational specialties more suited to their interests... or, more often, to avoid combat. College enrollment among young men took off at an unprecedented rate.

Initially, most young men supported the war. They grew up in the shadow of parents who survived the Great Depression and defeated the Axis powers during World War Two. Many of their family members served in Korea, and they understood that communism would never retreat on its own. It would only concede when a greater force was applied against it.

However, as many were eager to follow in the footsteps of previous generations, others considered Johnson's draft mandates a "death sentence." To this second group, the mandates were unjust commands that compelled them to risk life and limb in a faraway country for vague reasons they didn't understand. Some fled to neutral countries such as Canada, Mexico, or Sweden to avoid the draft. Some sought refuge in college or parental deferments. Others intentionally failed aptitude tests, while others engaged in outright resistance, such as protests and burning draft cards. Those with politically connected parents sought shelter in the National Guard and Reserves, comfortably assured that Johnson would not call on them to participate. Of the 27 million men eligible for the draft during the Vietnam War, more than half were deferred, exempted, or disqualified.[22]

The warriors of the Vietnam War were, on average, much younger than their forebears. The mean age for U.S. soldiers in Vietnam was nineteen, compared with twenty-six in World War Two. One irony of Vietnam was how the young men fighting and dying in Vietnam had no authentic voice in politics until 1971 when Congress changed the voting age from twenty-one to eighteen. Nobody cared how these young men felt about the war. Moreover, draftees received minimal training to prepare for Vietnam. Apart from basic combat and technical skills, soldiers knew very little about the South Vietnamese people, their culture and customs, religion, or community life.

The Legacy of Compromised Leadership

At the time of writing, we're more than fifty years removed from Johnson's passing, and our nation is approaching another tipping point. People of all cultural and political stripes can sense it. The United States of America is the longest-serving tenured government in world history. But when a nation moves in the wrong direction, the people's only recourse is to demand honesty and integrity from themselves and their leaders. Without firm public insistence on the truth, leaders will not make the hard decisions to change course. A storm is fast approaching and is already upon us because of our unwillingness to repent and unify.

In the more immediate sense, Johnson watched his political capital whittle away and deteriorate rapidly as the antiwar movement and counterculture gathered steam throughout 1966-68. He was caught between a rock and a hard place; he couldn't afford to lose in Vietnam and lacked the authority and credibility to rally the nation to finish the job. When the 1968 presidential race kicked off, Johnson famously said, "I shall not seek, and I will not accept, the nomination of my party for another term as your president."

By the time Johnson made this announcement, thousands of young American men had already died in a conflict with no clear objective, strategy, or timetable. Johnson's obstinacy and compromised integrity had come full circle; he couldn't even ask Americans to trust him to complete what he started. All Johnson could do was walk away without hope of comparison to President Roosevelt. In his post-presidency, Johnson battled failing health, political irrelevance, and multiple heart attacks before he died in 1973. Ironically, the Vietnam War outlived him.

Considering Johnson's example, wouldn't now be a good time for us all to come clean, tell the truth, and explore the vulnerable flip-side of lionheartedness? Wouldn't it be an excellent time to humble ourselves, shed light on our collective moral failures, and turn back to first principles? If you could reach back through time and show the leaders of America in the 1960s what havoc their dishonesty would wreak... would you do it to spare all those young men the horrors and savagery of death, suffering, and torment from war?

On America's 100th birthday, in his Centennial Address to Congress in 1876, President James A. Garfield issued a warning:

Now, more than ever before, the people are responsible for the character of their Congress. If that body is ignorant, reckless, and corrupt, it is because the people tolerate it. If it is intelligent, brave, and pure, it is because people demand these high qualities to represent them in the national legislature. If [one hundred years from now] the next centennial does not find us a great nation... it will be because those who represent the enterprise, the culture, and the morality of the nation do not aid in controlling the political forces.[23]

The message is clear: the survival of our nation depends on what we demand of ourselves and our leaders.

So What Do We Do?

It's abundantly clear that we, the people of God, can't afford to sit on the sidelines and be disengaged from the world around us, the political process, or even our local communities. But how do we engage without a national and cultural revival?

When we engage, what kind of character does the world experience? Do we become another group of people shouting slogans, hurling insults, and leveling accusations? If so, we shouldn't be surprised when neighbors tune us out. They already hear plenty of that from every angle and direction. If we do the same, we descend to the level of those who spewed venom at our warriors when they returned home from Vietnam.

Are we still following President Johnson's example? Do we distrust counsel from others? Do we show favoritism to specific groups based on superficial characteristics? Do we bend the truth and leverage people and institutions for our own benefit?

If so, we should not expect any reward—from God or man. Instead, we should expect to feel confused and despair about our service and sacrifice.

On the other hand, what could we unleash if we embrace a principled stand—with nothing to prove, nothing to hide, and nothing to fear?

What if the small moral choices we make in our own lives affect the larger picture? Isn't it worth at least *trying* to do things God's way after more than six decades of trying to manufacture our own morality and justify ourselves?

Even if it's just you and the rest of society doesn't change at all … for the peace of your soul and the integrity of your heart, it's worth examining your life. It's worth confessing your failures and bad decisions. It's worth offloading guilt, shame, regret, anger, bitterness, and frustration.

It's worth exploring the flip-side of lionheartedness… because, like President Johnson, the decisions you make based on your worldview carry enormous consequences—especially for people you love.

It's worth being able to stand your ground when the storm approaches. Courageous warriors who stand their ground are central to the Hope of War.

Chapter Four
America's War

There are always lessons to learn from drifting in uncharted waters. Initially, the situation may seem overwhelming. But by maintaining the proper perspective, you develop the skills you need in the moment. We can always find reasons for hope.

During the first six months of 1965, President Lyndon Johnson decided to "Americanize" the conflict in Vietnam. Practically, this meant the U.S. would intervene in a conflict we didn't understand, which had already spanned an entire generation – and we would do so by giving the enemy a say in how we went about it.

As a North Vietnamese ally, China warned the Johnson Administration early on that it would not permit a full-scale invasion of North Vietnam. Afraid of provoking an all-out war with a much larger communist nation, Johnson forfeited both invasion of Vietnam and sponsoring an anti-communist insurgency as strategies for defeating the enemy.

Stop for a moment and think of the folly of that decision, transplanted back to World War Two. What if, for fear of upsetting Adolf Hitler, President Franklin Roosevelt refused to invade Italy? What if the Allies had stopped in North Africa and waited for the Axis Powers to recuperate, rebuild their military, conquer Europe, and launch another full-scale invasion of Great Britain? You allow your *enemy* to decide when and where you're "permitted" to fight?!

I didn't grasp it at the time, but today, I see clear parallels from my experience with spiritual warfare as a Christian. In Vietnam, the U.S. fought blindfolded, against veteran foes on their home turf. Our opponents sneered at our discomfort with the horrors of war and used them as emotional blackmail during negotiations. They manipulated our internal conflict and compromise, to such an extent that our leaders lost all sense of purpose. In the end, the greatest military superpower in human history walked away and abandoned the effort, like they subsequently did in Iraq and Afghanistan.

Sadly, this too is nothing new. On the spiritual battlefield, believers do it all the time. Many believers do the same thing, despite being imbued with the Spirit of God—the greatest superpower in the entire universe.

The Iron Curtain of Southeast Asia

The nation of South Vietnam was artificial, in many ways, like East Germany after World War Two. Instead of an organically-formed nation with a unique history, South Vietnam was the result of a political compromise—a compromise between the Western Powers (the United States, France, and the United Kingdom) and the Eastern communist bloc (China and the Soviet Union) at the 1954 Geneva Conference. Vietnam got divided up the same way Germany did.

You could say the same is true for believers in Jesus, fighting against the principalities and powers of darkness in a world of illusions. Many "borders" we create are the results of *compromise*— deals with devils. Ignorant of our purpose and blind to the hostile forces that oppose it, we try to bargain for a safe, quiet, out-of-sight life. We settle for a fraction of what we rightfully own, and surrender without a fight. And then we're surprised to find that the enemy does not share our respect for the terms of the treaty!

Ho Chi Minh, the leader of North Vietnam, presented himself as a Vietnamese Nationalist. In reality, he was a cold-blooded communist. In the 1920s, Ho served as an undercover agent for Communist International, a network of agents and spies controlled by Joseph Stalin. In the 1930s, he took sanctuary in the Soviet Union, using the time to gain notoriety by supporting Stalin's oppressive policies. Ho also joined the Chinese Communist Party in the 1940s, when it received most of its cues from Moscow.[1] Ho owed his success to communist networks outside Vietnam.

By living abroad at length, Ho managed to survive when many other Vietnamese nationalists, non-communists, and communists ended up imprisoned or executed by the Colonial French (and later, by the Japanese) during World War Two. His loyalty to communism far surpassed his connection to Vietnamese heritage. Ho's "patriotism" toward Vietnam was a mere contrivance, a respectable cover for his real intentions.

Does any of this sound familiar if you've read or studied spiritual warfare? It's the same template Satan uses—masquerading as an angel of light!

When he gained power in North Vietnam, Ho followed the strategy he learned from Stalin and Mao Zedong: he terrorized the citizenry into accepting totalitarian rule. He launched a comprehensive purge of the country's intellectual and cultural talent and coerced the peasantry into servitude.[2]

Do you see the pattern yet? It's the same one used by Fidel Castro in Cuba, Kim Il-Sung in North Korea, and Robert Mugabe in Zimbabwe. And behind these tyrants is the prince of darkness, stirring the pot.

The Blind Leading the Blind

Believe it or not, the enemy has a plan for everyone – even if you stand on the side of freedom and human rights or are generally allied with the West. For every Castro or Kim, there is a Ferdinand Marcos, Francisco Franco, or Augusto Pinochet—who perhaps has better values than a communist... but who is still morally compromised or willing to resort to corruption, brutality, and hypocrisy so long as they get to stay in power.

In South Vietnam, that leader was Ngo Dinh Diem, a respectable, upper-class nationalist who resisted both the French and the Japanese during their occupations in Vietnam. Diem loosely embodies the tendency we all share to lower ourselves to the enemy's level—to "fight fire with fire." Diem waged an unremitting and brutal war on communists, as well as several religious sects. At first, leaders in Washington, D.C., were delighted by Diem's success, and American aid poured into South Vietnam.

But beneath the outward success of the Diem regime lay fatal flaws. A poor administrator who refused to delegate authority, Diem was pathologically suspicious of anyone outside his own family. His brother and close confidant, Ngo Dinh Nhu, controlled an extensive system of extortion, payoffs, and influence peddling through a secret network called the Can Lao. It planted clandestine members in every government bureau and military unit, as well as in schools, newspapers, and business.[3] To maintain control over the South Vietnamese population, Diem employed nepotism, favoritism toward Catholic groups (of which he and his family were members), and bribery of local political officials. When leaders are as vicious in the name of freedom as they are in the cause of tyranny, you can't blame the people they govern for simply wanting to hide—or rebel, given half the chance.

As with many leaders who fell to the communists—Juan Bautista in Cuba, Chiang Kai-shek in China, or the Russian tsars—it's not enough to be a leader that is "less corrupt than the next guy." It is *virtuous* leadership from leaders and citizens that makes a nation great. We despise virtue in U.S. politics today. It's one reason we get the leaders we do, which is exactly what Satan wants: blind, morally compromised citizens and leaders, one subservient to another, aiding and abetting his mission of destroying humankind.

President John F. Kennedy and his advisers believed Vietnam presented an opportunity to test the U.S.'s ability to conduct a "counterinsurgency" against communism. Kennedy agreed with the so-called "domino theory," which held that the fates of all Southeast Asian countries were closely linked. Communist success in one nation led to the fatal weakening of others. Success in Vietnam—in Kennedy's words, "the cornerstone of the free world in Southeast

Asia"—would provide evidence for allies and adversaries alike of U.S. resolve to prevent communist expansion in the Third World.[4]

Kennedy first had to deal with more pressing issues. These included the construction of the Berlin Wall and the Berlin airlift, conflicts between the Laotian government and the communist-led Pathet Lao, and the humiliating Bay of Pigs debacle in Cuba. Due to these other, more widely publicized crises, Vietnam fell into the background, even as it grew in importance.[5] Membership in Vietnam's communist National Liberation Front (NLF) expanded. Military setbacks to the Army of the Republic of Vietnam (ARVN) continued, and the infiltration rate from North Vietnam accelerated.

As South Vietnam deteriorated, Kennedy dispatched two key advisers, economist Walt W. Rostow and former Army chief of staff Maxwell Taylor, to Saigon in the fall of 1961. They concluded that the South Vietnamese government had neither the will nor the ability to turn the tide against the Viet Cong. They recommended an increase in U.S. assistance: equipment, such as helicopters and armored personnel carriers, and American advisers and technical experts embedded throughout the Vietnamese government and military. They also recommended a limited number of U.S. combat troops, in echo of a request from the Joint Chiefs of Staff.[6]

Aware of the consequences of losing another country to the communists, Kennedy was in the same "no man's land" he bequeathed to his successor. There was no viable exit from Vietnam, nor could Kennedy commit combat troops to war. So, he punted; he expanded the aid and guidance proposed in the Rostow-Taylor report. He also added a new four-star general position—Commander, U.S. Military Assistance Command Vietnam (USMACV)—in Saigon to guide the effort.

Aside from giving the communists more time and momentum, Kennedy's actions achieved little else.

Asymmetric War

Have you noticed how the kingdom of darkness doesn't fight fair? It is ruthless and vicious in direct combat, using anyone and anything for shelter, cover, or bargaining. The rest of the time, it wages campaigns of seduction and compromise. Many believers fall to the tactics primarily because of their own lack of commitment and understanding.

Despite American training and weapons, the ARVN was ill-suited to battle the insurgency of the Viet Cong. Their ranking officers, appointed based on family connections and political reliability, were often apathetic, incompetent, or corrupt—sometimes all three. With heavy American-style equipment, the ARVN was principally a road-bound force poorly configured to pursue Viet Cong units in swamps or jungles. Viet Cong agents easily penetrated the upper ranks of the ARVN in positions varying from drivers, clerks, and radio operators to senior headquarters officers. On the battlefield, the VC easily outmaneuvered the ARVN with guerrilla tactics and an abundance of cover in the jungle's foliage.[7]

U.S. military advisers responsible for developing and improving the ARVN also failed. They lacked knowledge of Vietnamese culture, language, and customs. They rarely spent more than twelve months in-country before returning home. You could say that even before President Johnson ordered U.S. warriors into combat, our level of commitment to Vietnam was half-hearted, and half-heartedness is the quickest path to compromise and seduction. You can't win hearts, minds, and souls when all you want to do is go home.

The first line of attack for the communists was the People's Liberation Armed Forces (PLAF), which you could loosely compare to the American Reserves and National Guard, or militia. At the base of the PLAF were village guerrilla units comprised of part-time combatants who lived at home and worked at their regular daily occupations. Their job was to persuade or intimidate their neighbors into supporting the NLF, protect its political apparatus, and harass the government, police, and security forces with booby traps, raids, kidnappings, and murders.[8]

The guerrilla forces also served as a recruiting agency for the PLAF. Above the guerrillas were the "regional forces"—full-time soldiers organized in a platoon (ten to twelve men) or company (170 men or less) that operated within the bounds of a province or region. These groups were more well-equipped and could operate throughout a province (regional forces) or even the country (main forces).[9]

The Viet Cong quickly learned to cope with the ARVN's new array of American weapons. Helicopters proved vulnerable to small-arms fire, while armored personnel carriers could be stopped or disoriented if their drivers or machine gunners were hit. Viet Cong troops survived many encounters because the South Vietnamese Army remained incompetent, faction-ridden, and poorly trained.

Diem and the Dominoes

By the summer of 1963, there were growing doubts around the world about the ability of the Diem government to prosecute the war. Members of Diem's family compounded the instability. U.S. intelligence suspected Diem's brother Nhu, a habitual opium user, of secretly negotiating with North Vietnam. Nhu's wife, better known to the world as Madame Nhu, wielded enormous influence, which she used to promote Roman Catholic social causes and ridicule the country's Buddhist majority.

In May, the Ngos became embroiled in a fatal quarrel with Buddhist leadership. Strikes and demonstrations by Buddhists in Saigon and Hue met with violence from the army and Nhu's security forces, leading to numerous arrests. The following month, a Buddhist monk, Thich Quang Duc, publicly doused himself with gasoline and set himself ablaze to protest Diem's repression. Sensational photographs of the event appeared on the front pages of major American newspapers the following morning.

Many students and members of the professional classes in South Vietnamese cities joined the Buddhists. After a series of brutal raids by government forces on Buddhist pagodas in August, a group of South Vietnamese generals secretly approached the U.S. government to determine how Washington might react to a coup to remove Diem. Officially, the U.S. remained neutral, but our embassy maintained contact with the dissident generals while abandoning the Ngos, who were captured and murdered by the army. On November 1, ARVN units seized control of Saigon, disarmed Nhu's security forces, and occupied the presidential palace.

Kennedy was assassinated less than two weeks after Diem's death, leaving Lyndon Johnson with a legacy of indecision and half-measures in Vietnam (not to mention a leadership vacuum). Johnson felt equally aware of the price of "losing" another country to communism. Still, he differed from his predecessor in one regard: when he won his first election in a landslide, he believed it gave him a mandate to resolve the issue. Johnson shared the view of most of his advisers, many of them Kennedy holdovers, that Vietnam was a test of U.S. Cold War resolve.[10] Determined to fulfill the American promise to South Vietnam, one of Johnson's first moves was to promote General William Westmoreland, a former superintendent of the U.S. Military Academy at West Point, to oversee the effort. He also increased the number of U.S. military personnel in Vietnam from 16,000 to 23,000.

The situation worsened between the Gulf of Tonkin Resolution and the U.S. presidential election in November 1964. The Saigon regime shuffled through a bewildering array of governing cliques and coalitions, some of which stayed in power for less than a month. In the countryside, even the best ARVN units seemed incapable of defeating the main forces of the Viet Cong. The communists began deliberately targeting U.S. military personnel and bases, starting with a mortar attack on the U.S. air base at Bien Hoa near Saigon in November.

General Westmoreland predicted the collapse of the South Vietnamese Army, and he recommended a rapid dispatch of U.S.

troops to prevent the collapse of the entire country. In July 1965, Secretary of Defense Robert McNamara confirmed the need for additional forces. Weeks later, Johnson took the final steps that would commit the United States to full-scale combat in Vietnam: he authorized the dispatch of 100,000 troops immediately, followed by an additional 100,000 the following year.[11]

During a televised news conference, Johnson publicly announced his decision to intervene in Vietnam. However, there was no official declaration of war, nor was there any effort to seek one from Congress. This departure from tradition prevented the country from being fully prepared for war. To make matters worse, the National Guard and military reserves were sidelined for political reasons. Invading North Vietnam was not an option, leaving America with limited strategic alternatives. It was like entering the battle with one hand behind our back and our shoelaces tied together. On a smaller scale, young warriors often make the same mistake. They rush into battle without preparation or considering the consequences of their actions.

Failures of leadership are nothing new. In fact, they're a recurring theme throughout every stage of history and in all civilizations and societies. The Bible is replete with stories of kings who made poor decisions based on fear, misunderstood their people, and faced severe consequences. The Scriptures also caution against the outcomes of bad choices from the people themselves. If we fail to learn from history, we risk repeating our mistakes. As philosopher George Santayana observed, "Those who cannot remember the past are condemned to repeat it."

Sad Days in Blue Springs

President Johnson's announcement of America's intervention in Vietnam had an enormous impact, including on several of my family members, close friends, and classmates. The announcement brought change that affected families, livelihoods, and futures at a speed similar to the social reforms Johnson shepherded through Congress.

The situation left us blindsided, holding the bag of a slew of new realities. As the adrenaline wore off and the hardships of fighting an undeclared war, which our leaders seemed "determined to lose," began to sink in – fatigue and social unrest followed.

Carl "Lynn" West, my uncle by marriage, was the first member of our family to fight in Vietnam. He served as a UH-1 Huey helicopter gunship pilot with the 173rd Airborne Brigade, the "Sky Soldiers." Lynn played an essential part in Operation *Hump*, which was a joint search-and-destroy mission carried out by the U.S. and Australian forces in November 1965. The operation occurred northeast of Bien Hoa, a sizable American air base in South Vietnam. During this operation, around 1,200 Viet Cong insurgents ambushed the 173rd Sky Soldiers, leaving forty-eight of them dead and many others wounded. (Forty years later, country singers Big & Rich memorialized this battle with their hit song, "The 8th of November.")

Lynn also fought in the Iron Triangle, a well-entrenched Viet Cong stronghold located north of Saigon. In January 1966, Lynn participated in Operation *Marauder*, the first U.S. military operation in the Plain of Reeds, an inland wetland in Vietnam's Mekong Delta containing several Viet Cong logistics bases. His final mission was Operation Attleboro, a massive operation that involved twenty-one Allied battalions and 22,000 troops—aimed to locate the Viet Cong and force them to fight.

During his tour of duty in Vietnam, Lynn earned numerous military decorations and accolades. He received two Distinguished Flying Crosses, the Bronze Star Medal, a Purple Heart, the Vietnam Cross of Gallantry, the Presidential Unit Citation, and twenty-seven Air Medals, which represented a staggering 675 hours of combat flight. Lynn's dedication to the cause and selfless service reflected the spirit of a hero who put others first, even in the face of danger.

When he returned home, Lynn confided in my brother Fred that he was deeply conflicted about the recognition he received for taking others' lives. He had volunteered to serve his country and fight for the freedom of the South Vietnamese people against the oppressive forces of communism, but he never expected to be awarded medals for his actions.

In a span of sixteen months, beginning in 1966, two of my close friends and a family acquaintance were killed in action. All of them were nineteen-year-old Marines. Private First Class (PFC) Dale Hutchings was killed while on patrol by an improvised explosive device near Tuy River Bridge on August 3, 1966. A sniper killed Corporal (CPL) Ronnie Reeder on January 29, 1967, in the same general area as Dale. My parents were acquainted with the family of PFC B. L. Murphy. I didn't know him personally, but I'm told he got caught in an enemy crossfire during an operation and was killed in a matter of minutes, along with thirty other Marines, on December 28, 1967. All three men died in the infamous Quang Nam Province, one of the bloodiest hot spots in all of South Vietnam. I spent time with Dale and Ronnie before they shipped out for the war. From what they shared, they believed they were doing the right thing.

The deaths of three of our own had a profound impact on Smithville. After all, we were just like other small communities across the country. We lauded our young men when they left comfort and safety to fight communism. We grieved as a family when they were killed. We comforted those who returned with haunted faces and battle scars. It was a hard time, and the shock and sorrow showed in our own faces and heaviness of heart.

A War on Five Fronts

General Westmoreland divided South Vietnam into four Tactical Combat Zones, referred to as "corps" or military regions:

- U.S. Marines ran I-Corps (pronounced "Eye" Corps), the northern part, near the demilitarized zone (DMZ) at Da Nang Airbase

- The Army operated II-Corps, headquartered at Pleiku, a market town in the Central Highlands near Camp Holloway, a U.S. Special Forces base.
- The Army also oversaw III-Corps, the largest zone, stretching from Saigon to the Cambodian border. III-Corps HQ was Tan Son Nhut Airbase, also the headquarters of the Republic of Vietnam Air Force (RVNAF)
- Finally, the South Vietnamese Army operated IV-Corps in the south. Spanning the marshlands of the Mekong River Delta, IV-Corps shared the U.S. airbase at Can Tho with South Vietnamese Army headquarters.[12]

I-Corps' territory was the central cultural and economic base for South Vietnam. It consisted of five provinces with a population of 2.6 million people: Quang Ti, Thua Thien, Quan Nam, Quang Tin, and Quang Ngai. It also contained two of South Vietnam's historical cities: Hue, the old imperial and cultural capital of Vietnam, and Da Nang, a large seaport city second in size only to Saigon. However, most of the population lived in narrow coastal areas or fertile river valleys, where they made a living either as fishermen, rice farmers, or both.[13]

The Fifth Front

The most troubling zone of the conflict was back home in the United States. As wars go, Vietnam bore little resemblance to previous American conflicts. While we experienced the same grief and mourning of our forebears every time we lost a warrior, this conflict divided the home front against one another. Psychologically, as time passed, I believe it made significant contributions to the destabilized, polarized, and hatred-driven world of today. It shook our confidence as a nation, radicalizing some and isolating others.

For the people of Smithville, the deaths of three beloved sons in relatively rapid succession changed our discussions about the war. Our resolve to support Johnson began to wane. The war clearly lacked goals and objectives, and the longer it went on, the more it seemed as though we were "fighting for the sake of fighting." Even in its later stages, the objective in Vietnam remained convoluted and ambiguous. Regardless of who held the White House, nobody wanted to face the consequences of a lengthy string of bad decisions.

Nobody wanted to admit that we were morally compromised as a nation, which is part of what makes modern American wars so hard to win. Nobody wants to connect today's cultural tailspin to ignorance and moral compromise. We've resisted the idea for more than six decades. Whether the enemy takes the face of communism, Islamic terrorism or the ongoing chaos of financial meltdowns and pandemics —God keeps trying to get our attention. But we don't listen, nor do we change how we live.

Most of us in modern Christendom are "checking out," standing on the sidelines, watching our freedoms vanish and looking the other way, hoping (a) we don't get hit and (b) nobody notices us. God wants to grow our character, but we're hiding in the bushes like our ancient ancestors, Adam and Eve.

Blindsided by Tragedy

I was crushed by the loss of my close friends, with whom I had spent so much time. Suddenly, I realized that Vietnam wasn't an abstract reality. It was real and ugly, and I was among the next group of young men in line to face its wrath. What seemed distant now lay on my doorstep, leaving a heavy burden of grief in its wake. It was another shock, sent to overturn my carefree assumptions that what happened to others would never happen to me.

With so many things requiring my energy and attention, I struggled to focus. I was moving quickly, but I wasn't sure if I was headed in the right direction, the one God intended for me. My father, sensing my inner turmoil and grief from losing my friends, offered some wise counsel. He said, "Larry, while we cannot control the length of our life on earth, we can determine its *depth*. Our acceptance in Christ is secure, and we are complete in Him. However, that doesn't mean we should sit back and watch the world go by. It's the exact opposite; we are called to serve others, just as Jesus did."

Dad's counsel as I grieved the death of my friends was authentic, offered from his combat experiences in the Navy during World War Two. It opened my eyes and helped me tackle my pain and grief more constructively. It stuck with me and left an indelible reminder that love is stronger than fear, life is stronger than death, and hope is stronger than despair.

Life on Earth is God's "schoolroom" to prepare us for eternity. We're expected to grow and become more like Him through our difficulties and challenges. We will always struggle with sin and failure... but by walking through them, we mature and perfect our faith. If we hold to these truths, we won't be easily discouraged when we face temptations, problems, and situations we don't understand. If we know we're here for God's purposes, we can follow the advice of Winston Churchill: "If you're going through hell, keep going."

Most of all, I learned that to find the Hope of War, we must be *reconciled*—to our purpose, to God's commands, and the reality of war in the first place. I don't know if President Johnson ever found reconciliation... but I did, and it made all the difference.

PFC Alvin "Dale" Hutchings, USMC, was the first from my hometown to be killed in Vietnam. Dale served with Mike Company, 3rd Battalion, 3rd Marine Regiment, 3rd Marine Division, III Marine Amphibious Force (MAF). On 3 August 1966, "M" Company was part of a search and destroy Mission about 5km south of the Marine Corps Base at Da Nang. Dale's squad, comprised of 13 men (three fire teams of 4 men each plus a squad leader), patrolled the riverbank near the Tuy Loan River Bridge. As they moved toward the Command Post (CP), they took fire from across the river, wounding one of the Marines. It was an attempt to move the remaining Marines toward a nearby field of land mines. The tactic worked; the Marines got hit by an explosive device positioned alongside the river bank – most likely, a hand-detonated land mine. The resulting explosion wounded six Marines outright, including Dale. The squad called for a MEDEVAC helicopter, and loaded the injured Marines aboard. Unfortunately, Dale died en route to the hospital. He was 19.

Corporal (CPL) Ronnie Ellis Reeder was the second young man from my hometown to die in Vietnam. Ronnie served with Alpha Company, 1st Battalion, 1st Marine Regiment, 1st Marine Division. From 1-31 January 1967, Ronnie's squad from Alpha Company attached to Hotel (H) Company, 2nd Battalion, 1st Marine Regiment. Ronnie died on Sunday, January 29, 1967, when his squad patrolled in advance of the main Marine force led by Captain Edward  J. Banks. H Company led a sweep for the enemy about 15km (+/- 10 miles) southwest of the Marine Base at Da Nang. Just before noon, as they approached the hamlet of Thuy Bo, the squad came under heavy fire from an estimated 400-man Viet Cong battalion. Ronnie's squad was quickly isolated by ambush. He ran point that day and was killed by an enemy sniper. Hearing enemy fire, the main Marine force quickly surged forward – only to be penned down behind numerous rice paddy dikes by heavy enemy fire. Ronnie and his entire squad of five Marines had all been killed. He was 19.

PFC B. L. Murphy, Jr., died in action in Vietnam on December 28. 1967. B. L. served with India Company, 3rd Battalion, 5th Marines, 1st Marine Division, 3rd Marine Amphibious Force. India Company was part of Operation Auburn, which took place between December 28th, 1967 and January 3, 1968 south of Da Nang. Go Noi Island, the epicenter of the battle, was located some 25km south of Da Nang to the west of infamous Highway One. The area directly north of the island was nicknamed "Dodge City" by the Marines because of the frequent ambushes and firefights there. The area was a stronghold for Viet Cong and North Vietnamese Army forces. The operation called for four Marine infantry companies to establish blocking positions along the railway tracks on Go Noi Island, while South Vietnamese forces swept east to west along Route 537 in hope of pushing the Viet Cong and NVA forces against the Marines. B. L.'s company arrived at Landing Zone Hawk around 11:30 a.m. on Dec. 28th. Within minutes after landing, B.L. and 17 other Marines died coming to the aid of another company pinned down by enemy fire. B. L. was 19.

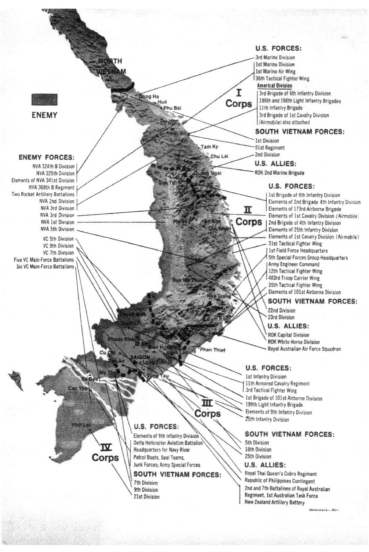

During the war, South Vietnam was divided into four Corps Tactical Zones, also called Military Regions, and the Special Capital Zone (Saigon area) for purposes of military operations. The four Corps Tactical Zones were identified as I-Corps (pronounced as "EYE" Corps), II-Corps, III-Corps and IV-Corps. Each was an administrative and command area for tactical operations. I-Corps was in the region nearest North Vietnam and adjacent to the DMZ. Map adapted from public domain.

Chapter Five
The Turning Point

**It's disappointing when reality falls short of our expectations.
But nothing falls short of God's expectations. He knows
everything, responds to our pain and hurt, and struggles with
the bigger picture in mind. We cannot prevent Him
from loving us even in our worst moments.[1]**

During a Harvard commencement address in 1978, acclaimed novelist and Soviet dissident Aleksandr Solzhenitsyn lamented how the West lost its civic courage. He warned, "From ancient times, the decline in courage has been considered the symptom of the end of civilization." He named Western culture's love of personal pleasure at the expense of public responsibility as the problem.[2]

By 1967, large numbers of Americans were opposed to the Vietnam War. Students, intellectuals, academics, and clergy opposed it on moral grounds. They lamented large numbers of civilian victims in both North and South Vietnam and blamed U.S. support of a corrupt, oppressive regime in Saigon. Organized protests became common, with youthful picketers converging at the White House and chanting, "Hey, hey, LBJ, how many kids did you kill today?"[3] A significant number of these protesters were my peers—young people in their late teens and twenties.

Public responsibility became a byword in the Sixties while hedonism and public disgrace rushed in to fill the void. Musical acts like The Beatles, The Doors, and Jimi Hendrix skyrocketed in popularity, with music celebrating the unraveling of Western civilization. Protesters lashed out at returning Vietnam veterans, calling us "baby killers" and spitting on us. It was ominous to see an entire generation "calling good 'evil,' and evil 'good,'" as the prophet Isaiah warned.

On October 21, 1967, protesters staged a massive anti-war march in Washington, D.C., Led by the National Mobilization Committee to

End the Vietnam War, which drew more than 100,000 attendees. They ranged from middle-class professionals and clergy members to hippies and black activists. A concert performance by counterculture folk singer Phil Ochs galvanized the initial rally at the Lincoln Memorial, followed by a series of speeches from activists. (Hollywood later dramatized this event in the 1994 movie *Forrest Gump*, where the protagonist, a Vietnam veteran, got roped into giving a speech alongside radical activist Abbie Hoffman.)

A crowd of 50,000 people marched across the Potomac River to the Pentagon, where they sparked a confrontation with U.S. paratroopers from the 82nd Airborne Division, who guarded the building. The demonstrations polarized the nation and produced a famous photograph of a protester placing flowers in a paratrooper's rifle. Increasing casualties and the lack of strategy in Vietnam persuaded many Americans that President Lyndon Johnson had failed. He'd forced the U.S. military to fight with both hands tied behind their backs. Polls showed less than fifty percent of citizens had a favorable view of how Johnson handled the war.[4]

In Hanoi, communist leaders also grew impatient with the war. As Ho Chi Minh aged, Le Duan became the primary decision-maker in the North Vietnamese government. Le understood that a long, protracted conflict would not work, regardless of how much support they received from China or the Soviet Union. General Nguyen Chi Thanh, supreme commander of communist forces in South Vietnam, shared Duan's opinion. Both men encouraged aggressive action to alter the direction of the war.

Though buoyed by their ability to hold their own against more numerous and better-armed opponents, North Vietnam didn't want endless, unresolved military conflict. Observing the steady flow of U.S. troops into South Vietnam, they decided to break the stalemate psychologically. Their strategy was to sow enough discontent in South Vietnam to collapse the regime of its leader, Nguyen Van Thieu. They hoped to convince the United States it could not win the war so that they could absorb South Vietnam under their rule once the U.S. left.

The Collapse of U.S. Resolve

In October, communist forces launched diversionary attacks against U.S. bases at Dak To and Loc Ninh. The objective was to distract attention from the upcoming offensive and draw U.S. forces into the open, away from major population centers. On January 21, 1968, two North Vietnamese artillery divisions bombarded the U.S. Marine garrison at Khe Sanh, near the border with Laos. For the next seventy-seven days, the Marines and South Vietnamese fought off an intense siege—one of the most protracted, bloodiest battles of the war.[5]

During this time, U.S. commanders in Saigon received intelligence that North Vietnam and the Viet Cong were preparing for a major campaign. The Khe Sanh offensive came shortly after broadcasts from the clandestine "Liberation Radio" network. The Alliance of National, Democratic, and Peace Forces—an urban front group established by the Viet Cong—encouraged the South Vietnamese to rebel against the Saigon government.[6]

General William Westmoreland believed the radio broadcasts were connected to the attack on Khe Sanh. He perceived them as a part of a larger strategy aimed at gaining control of the northernmost regions of South Vietnam. The communists wanted leverage before they would enter peace negotiations.

The U.S. responded with Operation *Scotland*. Westmoreland strengthened the Marine garrison at Khe Sanh. He stockpiled ammunition and refurbished the base's airstrip in preparation for an attack. President Johnson agreed with Westmoreland's assessment and ordered that Khe Sanh must be held at all costs. Westmoreland ordered a massive bombardment of suspected North Vietnamese artillery locations in the hills surrounding Khe Sanh.[7]

Johnson, Westmoreland, and other administration officials believed Khe Sanh was the enemy's primary target. By rushing to protect it, they ignored signs of communist buildup in other areas of South Vietnam. This would prove to be a colossal mistake with dire consequences. While their response to Khe Sanh took its toll on the enemy, it also revealed significant weaknesses for the U.S. and South Vietnam.

Public support for President Johnson's handling of the war continued to decline. More than two years after the first large wave of U.S. troops landed in Vietnam, Johnson had yet to seek Congress' approval for a declaration of war or to articulate what victory would look like. His goals in Vietnam included preventing the expansion of communist influence in Southeast Asia, strengthening the United States' position as a global superpower, and establishing a free, independent, and prosperous South Vietnam. They *sounded* nice... but he never specifically articulated what he meant by them or what it would look like if we accomplished them.

Did Johnson assume we would win because we were much bigger than North Vietnam? If so, it was a classic blunder of spiritual warfare, like David versus Goliath. Except, in this case, *we* looked like Goliath! Everyone knew who *should* have had the upper hand and who should have been crushed... but as Ecclesiastes reminds us, "The race is not always to the swift, nor the battle to the strong."

Johnson's objectives sounded nice, but they were vague. The lack of clarity among American leaders and the instability of the Saigon government put them even further out of reach. Evidence exists that Johnson recognized this as early as 1965, but it didn't matter. In a memo to the president that year, Defense Secretary McNamara wrote that while the war progressed well from a combat perspective, with thousands of enemy fighters being killed every month... its political dimension was in shambles. South Vietnam remained dysfunctional throughout the entire conflict. McNamara observed that "corruption is widespread," "real government control is confined to enclaves," and "there is rot in the fabric."[8]

For the remainder of Johnson's presidency, the protests and anti-war movement gained even more momentum. By the end of March, Johnson announced he would not seek re-election. A few days after his announcement, Dr. Martin Luther King, Jr. was assassinated in Memphis, Tennessee. Two months after King's death, Senator Robert F. Kennedy, brother of the former president, was assassinated in Los Angeles. Four months after that, protesters overran the Democratic National Convention in Chicago with a riot. This was a considerable departure from the unity, solidarity, and cooperation of previous American wars.

The Turning of the Tide at Tet

Tet is a highly anticipated celebration in Vietnamese tradition and plays a vital role in community life. It marks the lunar New Year and honors the country's ancestral past. Until 1968, South Vietnam, North Vietnam, and Viet Cong forces observed an informal truce during this period. But that year, General Vo Nguyen Giap, the North Vietnamese military commander, chose January 31st (the beginning of the Tet holiday) to launch coordinated surprise attacks to break the stalemate in Vietnam. Strategically, Tet was timed perfectly—half of the South Vietnamese military and the national police would be on leave. The Saigon government and its army were utterly unprepared for a nationwide wave of attacks.

General Giap believed an all-or-nothing effort by North Vietnamese and Viet Cong forces would trigger the collapse of the South Vietnamese military and incite discontent and rebellion among the people. Skilled at reading between the lines, he calculated that the alliance between South Vietnam and the United States was fragile and that the offensive would drive a wedge between the two governments. Eventually, American leaders would abandon their defense of South Vietnam.[9]

Meanwhile, General Westmoreland and his intelligence officials at MACV were too fixated on the strategy of attrition and "body counts" to recognize the ploy of the Dak To, Loc Ninh, and Khe Sanh border battles. Westmoreland saw them as opportunities to lure the enemy into the open, where the full might of the U.S. military could be brought to bear. He may have considered them a chance to avenge the

French defeat at the Battle of Dien Bien Phu. But whatever he thought, he did not perceive them as distractions.

The intro to the Tet Offensive began in the early hours of January 30, 1968. More than 70,000 North Vietnamese and Viet Cong troops launched a series of coordinated assaults on over one hundred locations across South Vietnam—big cities, regional capitals, and provincial hamlets. Within the first twenty-four hours, they attacked strategic targets like the presidential palace, Saigon's Tan Son Nhut Airport, and the city of Hue, the former seat of emperors. Fighting ensued for several days, with one wave of attacks after another. Some fighting even took place in the U.S. Embassy courtyard.[10]

Technically, the Tet Offensive was a military failure for the Viet Cong. American and South Vietnamese troops regrouped quickly, repelled the attackers, and killed as many as 40,000 soldiers. They subdued the embassy invaders within hours, depleted the Viet Cong's regular units beyond recovery, and crippled their political infrastructure.

But like Afghanistan, the Vietnamese have a long history of resisting outside forces, regardless of the death count. It's one reason France walked away from Indochina as a colony a decade earlier. Ironically, the Tet Offensive became a turning point—not militarily on the ground, but in U.S. domestic politics, policy, and public opinion. If Nazi Germany had their "D-Day" in World War II, the U.S. effort in Vietnam had its Tet Offensive. The attack caused substantial doubt about the war's direction. Over 500,000 American troops, three years of fighting, and tens of thousands of casualties achieved nothing more than a prolonged and bloody stalemate.[11] The North and the Viet Cong had achieved their primary objective. It was now a matter of time before the U.S. came to grips with their defeat.

For What It's Worth

Despite the media drumbeat about the Vietnam War, racial tensions, antiwar protests, and other issues of the day, I managed to graduate from high school in May 1967. It was a significant accomplishment, and that summer, I was thrilled to secure my first real job outside of working on our family farm. My uncle, Roger Underwood, hired me to help lay natural gas main and service lines in a small lake resort town in Glenwood, Minnesota. At the time, my brother Fred already worked for the same company as a foreman of several crews in Grand Island, Nebraska, under Roger's supervision.

I found my first three weeks on the job frustrating. A breakup with my high school sweetheart after graduation stung me more than I cared to admit. I pretended it didn't matter, but the pain of my first failed relationship took me by surprise. I hadn't expected the emotional fallout and had no idea how to deal with it. At work, this meant I required constant supervision. Roger expected me to perform like my brother, but as you know... Fred and I viewed life differently. My performance issues cratered on the day I damaged Roger's new welding truck as I backed out of a side street. I remember his stern rebuke over the incident as if it were yesterday: "You would think that a farm boy like you would know to look both ways when backing a truck!" On-the-job safety was the last thing on my mind; I was focused on everything *but* work.

Whether you fought in Vietnam or worked on natural gas pipelines (as I did), disappointment and failure are natural, unavoidable parts of the pathway to maturity. During these seasons, we may feel tempted to think, "My best days are behind me," or "It's all downhill from here."

The truth is more complicated. Failure and disappointment expose our assumptions and naivete, but that doesn't mean we must run away and never show our faces again.

At any point during his term in office, President Johnson could have admitted that he'd made poor decisions based on the wrong criteria. I know I did; eventually, I conceded that I was used to "coasting" through life, oblivious to reality, unprepared for what came along. You can acknowledge it today as a young active-duty warrior or an aged veteran. None of us can see the whole "picture" of our lives. It's okay ... and that's why we need Jesus' eyes.

At the same time, we all reach "turning points" where we must leave familiar settings and venture into the unknown, where we learn to see more of the complete picture than before. If we pass up opportunities to gain perspective and input from older, wiser, and more experienced people, these turning points can backfire and become even worse. Just because God doesn't show us the "full" picture doesn't mean He won't show us *more* of it today than He did yesterday.

When we move beyond our familiar settings, we need a direction or goal for our lives. I hadn't thought about either of those, so I succumbed to the "pull" of my previous life as though it were gravity. This, too, is part of the human experience. Wherever we go without vision, we "default" back to old ways—even ways we dislike. Working for Roger helped me move on from Smithville, but at the time, I didn't feel sure I wanted to leave. When I left the city limits, I gave little thought as to why I went—besides finding a job and making money. Of course, I needed an income, but I also required vision and direction for my life. Fortunately, Roger saw this and helped me grow and mature, freeing me from the emotional ties that held me back.

I felt embarrassed for damaging Roger's truck and not completing the expected work. But after he gave me my well-deserved scolding, he invited me to dinner at his house, where he also gave me the perspective and insight I needed.

He spoke about developing a work ethic and how it could help me to stand out. He taught me about self-awareness, sharing how I could access more opportunities by understanding my unique talents and personality traits. In construction, he told me, something else *always* needs to be done. Equipment needs refueling, lubrication, and cleaning. Everything requires thinking ahead, preparing for the next step, applying the right skills, and awareness of when to act versus when to wait.

Read that last paragraph again. If you've let life carry you along and it's led you to dark places in your soul, *remember this principle*! We will ALWAYS have more work to do and more perspective and insight to gain. Anything you go through will eventually end… but our need to grow, improve, and mature in handling life's challenges will last throughout our lifetimes.

That night at Roger's house became a turning point in my life. It changed my attitude and gave me the following "download" of today's perspective. I went back to work the following day, determined to make that "one small change" I talked about in the first chapter. From that day forward, when it came to working hard, I *attacked* work with a vengeance, giving it 110 percent effort, every day. I resolved to "over-deliver" for my uncle and redeem the ways I'd let him down. For a young man, few things feel as satisfying as the end of a hard day's work, knowing you gave it everything you've got.

We Who Served

These are the names of those I know and love, who went to Vietnam before, alongside, and behind me.

My brother, Fred, enlisted in the U.S. Navy as a Seabee under their Advanced Petty Officer Procurement Program, which based military rank on construction skills and practical experience rather than time in the service.

Fred completed his initial military training at the Naval Construction Battalion Center in Gulfport, Mississippi. Then, he deployed to Vietnam as an equipment operator for Naval Mobile Construction Battalion 121. Their mission was to build infrastructure to support the U.S. and its allies. Seabees, trained in combat and construction, often worked amid the thick of combat while in Vietnam. The Vietnam Veterans Memorial in Washington, D.C., commemorates the names of eighty-five Seabees who died in the war. It pays tribute to their motto, "We build, we fight," symbolized by their logo of a bee holding a wrench, a hammer, and a machine gun.

When I finished the construction season in Nebraska, I learned that my uncle, Lynn West, was on his way to Vietnam for a second tour. This time, he would fly Huey Cobra gunships for the 235th Armed

Helicopter Company, also known as the "Delta Devils," located at the Army airfield near Can Tho City in the Mekong Delta (IV-Corps).

On February 2, 1968, a routine nighttime "firefly" mission in the Mekong Delta took a tragic turn for Lynn. They diverted the mission to provide backup and support to a South Vietnamese army unit under severe attack from a Viet Cong battalion. The enemy ambushed Lynn's helicopter, killing everyone on board. Lynn's loss left a deep void in our family, and we were proud of his bravery and sacrifice. As a teenager, I admired Lynn for his self-confidence, love for his family, passion for the outdoors, and sense of duty. I wasn't ready to lose him. I imagined my family had an exceptional immunity to the dangers of war, but Lynn's death changed that.

My cousins, Gary Wayne Cripps and Hugh Riley Turner, also deployed to Vietnam. Gary worked as a trained truck driver in Fort Huachuca, Arizona, but when he reached Vietnam, he was assigned as a grenadier (M-79 grenade launcher) in Bravo Company, 1st Battalion, 8th Infantry Regiment, 4th Infantry Division. As the U.S. Marines are fond of saying, "Every man is a rifleman."

Gary was critically injured during the "Nine Days in May" battle near Pleiku on the Cambodian border. He shielded his squad leader from enemy fire, saving his life. After recovering from his wounds at Fort Gordon, Georgia, Gary received the Silver Star for bravery from General Walter Richardson, the post commander.

Hugh Riley underwent advanced combat engineering training at Fort Hood, Texas, before deploying to Vietnam with the 326th Engineer Battalion as part of the 1st Brigade, 101st Airborne Division.[14] The 1st Brigade stood on its own until the rest of the division arrived in December 1967. It consisted of ten battalions of airmobile infantry, six battalions of artillery, and an aviation group–three battalions of assault helicopters and gunships. General Westmoreland assigned the 101st near the border with Laos to block the North Vietnamese from resupplying Viet Cong forces in the South.

When the division arrived at Cam Ranh Bay in South Vietnam, Westmoreland and outgoing Ambassador Maxwell Taylor (formerly a four-star general) welcomed the command. Shortly after arrival, the paratroopers performed an airborne demonstration jump to honor their guests. Both Taylor and Westmoreland had previously served as 101st Division commanders, known during World War II as the "Screaming Eagles." The 101st has a rich and storied history, including participating in combat jumps during the invasion of Normandy on June 6th, 1944, and the subsequent Market Garden airborne operation in the Netherlands. Later, the division secured its place in military history at Bastogne during the Battle of the Bulge.[12]

The 326th Engineer Battalion arrived in Vietnam on November 24, 1967, and supported the 101st during Operation *Somerset Plain* in the Central Highlands. Later, they followed division units to the A Shau Valley, located further north of Phu Bia, a prominent allied base with a massive airfield. Due to its strategic location, the enemy frequently targeted Phu Bia with mortar attacks. One such battle took place on August 30, 1967, where Viet Cong forces assaulted the base, damaging thirteen helicopters, killing two Navy Seabees, and injuring thirty-two other sailors and marines.

Hugh Riley returned home in the spring of 1969, barely escaping the infamous battle for Ap Bia Mountain, also known as "Hamburger Hill." The fighting killed an estimated 630 North Vietnamese. The U.S. lost seventy-two soldiers, and 372 were wounded. Although the battle had no strategic value for either side, MACV officials claimed it to be a substantial victory based on the number of enemies killed. However, the enemy returned and occupied the hill within weeks after the Americans abandoned it. Criticism of the battle's senselessness and photos published in *Life* magazine of U.S. soldiers killed during the fight exacerbated the outrage.[13]

My close friend, Larry Caldwell, arrived in Vietnam around the same time as Lynn. Larry was assigned to the 110th Transportation Combat Support Unit in Saigon. He was there during the Tet Offensive and witnessed many of the unfolding battles in the streets of the city that claimed the lives of American and South Vietnamese soldiers. Another good friend, Danny "Snowball" Young, worked as a military policeman (MP) to protect Bien Hoa Air Base. Danny was wounded twice while coming to the aid of fallen comrades.

Billy Adcock, also known as Anthony, graduated in my high school class. We took woodworking lessons together. During the summer, my mother sent me an article in the *Smithville Review* that mentioned Anthony was serving in Vietnam as a member of Charlie Company, 1st Battalion, 18th Infantry Regiment, 1st Infantry Division. The "Big Red One," as the division was known, participated in the D-Day invasions during World War II. They also earned the nickname "Bloody Red One" for the heavy battles they fought to force Germany's surrender.

In high school, I played football alongside Norman Young, an exceptional athlete with a strong sense of duty. Norman didn't wait for the draft; he enlisted in the United States Air Force. He served at the Phan Rang Airfield in the south-central coastal region of Vietnam, close to the U.S. military base at Cam Ranh Bay.

Norman's childhood friend and former neighbor, Danny Young (no relation), got drafted in the summer. Within a few months, he deployed to Vietnam, where he joined Charlie Company, 4th Battalion, 9th Infantry Regiment, 25th Infantry Division. At twenty-two years old, Danny and forty-eight fellow soldiers died during a search and destroy mission on March 2, 1968, in an area northeast of Saigon. Caught in the crossfire of RPGs, machine guns, and rifle fire, Danny stayed in the fight until the end. He posthumously received the Silver Star for bravery.

PFC Anthony Adcock died on October 4, 1968, during an early morning Viet Cong mortar attack in an area known as "Hobo Woods," a well-known enemy haven. His courage and dedication to duty earned him a posthumous Bronze Star Medal.

Darkest Hours

Many of the losses of the Tet Offensive stemmed from General Westmoreland's refusal to acknowledge that he had a flawed plan for Khe Sanh. He ignored the contingencies some of his staff suggested and pressed forward. Westmoreland's strategy relied too heavily on U.S. firepower and aerial bombardment of enemy units. Rather than capturing and holding territory, he aimed to inflict more losses on the communists than they could withstand. He failed to recognize the enemy's expertise in guerrilla warfare and underestimated their nationalist zeal and will to fight. Along with others in the Johnson administration, Westmoreland could not see the North Vietnamese war effort for what it was: a nationalist struggle fueled by passion and conviction.[14]

After the Tet Offensive, Johnson should have relieved Westmoreland of his post. Instead, he was promoted to Chief of Staff of the U.S. Army, with General Creighton Abrams succeeding him as commander of MACV. Westmoreland's influence declined during the administration of President Richard Nixon, and he eventually retired in 1972. He launched a failed bid for public office and retreated into obscurity. Late in his life, he developed Alzheimer's disease and died in 2005.

As for President Johnson, 1968 became the death knell of his political career. On March 31st, he informed the American public he would not seek nomination for re-election. His vice president, Hubert Humphrey, picked up the standard for the Democratic Party, only to be defeated in a three-way race against segregationist George Wallace and the eventual winner, President Nixon.

I don't recall seeing it this way, then, but the "changing of the guard" should serve as a sobering reminder for all of us. Just because the names and faces have changed doesn't mean God has changed His strategies for getting our attention. In fact, the more the world changes… the more we must rely on things that *never* change, and one of those is that God always desires our growth and maturity as His followers.

For both Presidents Johnson and Nixon, their stories had disappointing endings—moral compromises, tarnished legacies, and unresolved conflicts. Some of us might have hoped that a new president would change the story toward a brighter future. If we did, we were wrong to do so. True change toward a brighter future always begins from within the soul of a human being. God humbled both of those men, and he humbled all of us as well.

If, today, you think electing one candidate over another will "fix" everything that's broken in society … you're mistaken. Change must come from *inside you*—it can't come from anywhere else. Don't wait for the situation around you to improve. *You must improve*, and the situation will follow.

If I had those years to do all over again, I would have viewed those changes in presidential leadership as signs that more exercises in maturity lay ahead, as I do today. My service in Vietnam began after Johnson's presidency, under a different commander-in-chief who promised to bring "peace with honor" and end the war.

But God had a much better plan for me. He would show me that I could take more "hits" than I thought possible and keep pursuing Him —that I could keep growing, even when everything around me seemed hopeless.

His plan was to teach me the Hope of War.

My brother, Petty Officer Second Class (E-5) Fred W. Cripps. Fred served in Vietnam with Naval Mobile Construction Battalion 121 (NMCB 121) from 1968-69. This same battalion, Naval Construction Battalion 121 (NCB-121), was deployed to the Pacific during World War II to support the United States Marines. In October 1968, the battalion arrived at Camp Wilkinson near Phu Bai, South Vietnam. NMCB-121 built infrastructure to support the U.S. and its allies.

SP/4 Danny S. Young was drafted in the summer of 1967 and sent to South Vietnam. He served in Charlie Company, 4th Battalion, 9th Infantry Regiment, 25th Infantry Division. On March 2, 1968, a company of Viet Cong soldiers ambushed Charlie 4-9 at a bridge on Route 248 close to Hoc Mon village, 14km (8.4 miles) northwest of Saigon. Forty-nine Americans perished, and twenty-eight others were wounded in less than eight minutes. The enemy concealed themselves in prepared positions and used small arms, automatic weapons, and Claymore mines. Gunships, artillery, and air strikes supported Charlie Company, but sniper fire by rear guard elements prevented Alpha, Bravo, and Delta companies from reinforcing them. Danny fought bravely until he was mortally wounded by grenade fragmentation near the Route 248 Bridge. He posthumously received the Silver Star for his bravery on that infamous day. Danny was 22.

PFC Billy Anthony Adcock bravely served in Charlie Company, 1st Battalion, 18th Infantry, 1st Infantry Division, famously known as the 'Big Red One.' During a search and destroy mission in the North Vietnamese Army (NVA) sanctuary called the 'Hobo Woods,' Anthony's platoon encountered intense resistance, which ultimately led to his untimely demise. His company boarded choppers on October 3rd, and the following day, the NVA launched a deadly mortar attack at about 5:20. Despite the lack of cover, Anthony and his comrades bravely fought back. However, the enemy's proximity was dangerously close, and the mortar shells rained down on them without mercy. Anthony's life was tragically cut short on October 4, 1968, which happened to be his mother's birthday. Anthony was 19.

On July 6th, 1965, Company A of the 326th Engineer Battalion was sent to South Vietnam as part of the 1st Brigade Task Force of the 101st Airborne Division. The rest of the battalion joined them in Vietnam on August 3, 1967. While in Southeast Asia, the 326th Engineer Battalion supported the Division by primarily focusing on construction in the A Shau Valley and building facilities and roadways to aid the South Vietnamese incursion into Laos. Despite being assigned huge construction tasks, the engineers were always ready to help the combat troops. They built ports and depots, constructed airfields and airstrips out of jungle and mountain plateaus, repaired roads and bridges, and constructed bases. Because of these efforts, ground combat troops, alongside their supporting engineers, could fight the enemy from well-established bases.

This is a photo of my cousin, Hugh Riley Turner, a member of A Company, 326th Engineer Battalion, attached to the 101st Airborne Division at Camp Eagle near Phu Bai, South Vietnam. This was when the United States military involvement in South Vietnam peaked. Camp Eagle, also known as LZ El Paso and LZ Tombstone, was the primary US Army base for the 101st Airborne Division, located southeast of Hue, the ancient imperial capital of Vietnam in the central part of the country.

This is a photograph of my cousin, Gary Cripps, receiving the Silver Star award while recovering from his wounds at Fort Gordon, Georgia. Gary was injured during the "Nine Days in May" battle near Pleiku on the Cambodian border. He sustained injuries while protecting his squad leader by shielding him with his own body against continuous enemy fire.

My uncle, Army Captain Carl "Lynn" West, receives the Distinguished Flying Cross for his heroic actions during aerial flight. This ceremony took place at Bien Hoa Airfield in Vietnam in January 1966. Shaking Lynn's hand is Major General Ellis W. Williamson, the first commander of the famous 173rd Airborne Brigade (Separate). General Williamson was from North Carolina and participated in the D-Day Normandy landings and the Inchon landing during the Korean Conflict. This was the first of three Distinguished Flying Cross awards Lynn earned before being killed in action on February 2. 1968, during a late-night air assault mission. Family photo.

Chapter Six
Embracing The Warrior's Path

Faithfully doing small things prepares you for more significant opportunities. Who you are on the inside is more important than who you pretend to be on the outside.

By the end of 1968, the Cold War Agreement undergirding American participation in Vietnam crumbled to pieces. The polls of the day revealed greater awareness of the Vietnamese situation among the public than among certain presidential candidates. Unfortunately, because Richard Nixon refused to participate, the candidates never explained their plans in a presidential debate format. However, most Americans believed Vietnam was the nation's primary concern. There was a sense of urgency that the war needed to end and a vague consensus among the people on how to go about it.

During his election campaign, Nixon devised a strategy to conclude the war. First, the South Vietnamese had to take charge of combat operations. This would allow U.S. forces to gradually reduce their levels and withdraw. It became known as "Vietnamization." Secondly, the U.S. applied constant pressure on North Vietnam (bombing and blockades) while negotiating the possibility of a peace treaty with them. Nixon also sought assistance from the Soviet Union, hoping their influence over North Vietnam would encourage negotiations and peacefully resolve the war.

Once the war ended, Nixon proposed ending the military draft and transitioning the entire U.S. military to an all-volunteer force. This was meant to ease the social and political tensions the war stirred up and ensure the armed forces were full of volunteers committed to serving their country willingly. Overall, Americans received Nixon's strategy well. They were eager to see an end to the Vietnam War. Did he have a perfect plan? No, but it revealed a departure from previous policies and a new chapter in the nation's approach to the war going forward.[1]

The Change of the Guard

During the 1968 presidential campaign, only two candidates spoke about a traditional military victory in Vietnam: Governor George Wallace and retired Air Force General Curtis LeMay. But their pledges demonstrated more rhetoric than anything else; they offered no serious, practical plans for accomplishing the goal. Except for nuclear weapons, Wallace proposed using "all the military ability we have, including air and naval power" to secure victory. The press and the public concluded that Nixon's "peace with honor" policy was a more promising approach.[2]

The anti-communist fervor and hawkish rhetoric of prior election seasons had waned or vanished altogether. According to the polls, the American public was more interested in the White House and Congress finding ways to end U.S. involvement in the war than anything else.

During the election year, *Life* magazine dispatched its Vietnam correspondents around the country to interview some three hundred men and women in the service about the election and the war. Although many soldiers they interviewed had not reached voting age, they were well-informed about the election, albeit unconvinced its outcome would make any difference in Vietnam.

The majority of those interviewed opposed any cessation of bombing in North Vietnam. They believed it was crucial to maintain the pressure on the enemy and disrupt efforts to target American troops. The interview participants emphasized the need to stand up to communism in Vietnam and prevent its spread. Most of them preferred Nixon, admired Bobby Kennedy, and showed surprising sympathy towards President Lyndon Johnson. But they primarily focused on finishing the job and surviving in Vietnam.[3]

In July, General Creighton W. Abrams succeeded William Westmoreland as the top commander of all U.S. forces in Vietnam. Renowned for his leadership skills as a battle tank commander during World War Two, Abrams led the rescue of the encircled 101st Airborne

Division at Bastogne during the Battle of the Bulge. His skill earned him two Distinguished Service Crosses, the nation's second-highest award for valor. (Modern tank soldiers with the U.S. Army should know the name "Abrams" well, particularly if they serve aboard the Army's M-1 "Abrams" tank.)

As the new MACV commander, Abrams joined forces with Ambassadors Ellsworth Bunker and William E. Colby. Bunker had served as a chief diplomat to South Vietnam since 1967 and displayed a keen intellect, superb negotiating skills, and modesty unusual for a foreign service officer. Colby worked as a career CIA officer who had previously served as the Agency's Chief of Station, Saigon, and then as the head of the CIA's Far East Division.[4]

The new leaders approached Vietnam with a fresh perspective, a three-part strategy for an outcome the American public could accept. They combined conventional and counterinsurgency methods across the four combat tactical zones. They chose an alternate metric for measuring progress to replace Westmoreland's "body counts." This meant they could use military assets more effectively and reduce casualties. Finally, they planned to stabilize the South Vietnamese government and its armed forces, which would reduce the need for U.S. support.

On October 31st, President Johnson declared a halt to bombing in North Vietnam and announced that peace negotiations in Paris would begin. These later became known as the "Paris Peace Accords."

In the short term, Johnson's decision had the potential to impact the election's outcome. It sparked intense debates and discussions across the country; many viewed it as a strategic move by Johnson to boost his party's chances of retaining control of the White House. Nixon's campaign hinged on a promise to end the Vietnam War, and he worried that Johnson's announcement could steal his thunder and diminish his chances of winning the presidency. It failed to do so.

Vietnamizing the Americanized War

On November 5th, Nixon became the 37th President of the United States. He won the election with a plurality—43.4 percent of the popular vote, defeating Vice President Hubert Humphrey (42.7 percent) and Wallace (13.5 percent). The public wanted to finish the Vietnam War, and it wanted a clear policy direction with timelines and objectives. Nobody wanted to hear more about increasing troop levels or escalating combat. As far as most Americans were concerned, the war needed phasing out.

Following Nixon's inauguration, Abrams set about the business of implementing Vietnamization—the antidote to Johnson's "Americanization"—and a steady decrease in U.S. involvement. Abrams based his strategy on the "one-war" concept: fostering political-military relations, disrupting the shadow government of South Vietnam (the communists), and spreading information rather than engaging in direct combat. He aimed to win the hearts and minds of the populace under a legitimate government rather than attrition of the enemy.[5]

Under Abrams' leadership, the military weakened the enemy's capabilities by attacking its logistical bases in South Vietnam and neighboring Cambodia and Laos.[6] Abrams gradually shifted American strategy from search-and-destroy operations to defending the population of South Vietnam. He presided over a vast augmentation of the South Vietnamese armed forces, leaving them with one of the largest and most well-equipped armies in the world—at least, on paper. (The numbers didn't correspond to reality.)

Abrams' approach helped deter the steady advance of North Vietnam into the South. His clear-and-hold, small-unit war of pacification strategy shifted U.S. military tactics and changed how we fought for the remainder of the conflict.

For all the unraveling it caused, the Tet Offensive produced some positive results for the Saigon regime. Tet exposed the South Vietnamese population to the brutality of the Viet Cong and North

Vietnamese Army. In places like the ancient imperial capital of Hue, the battle lasted one month and two days. It was one of the longest, bloodiest fights of the entire war, and it killed thousands of people. Enemy forces in the City of Hue killed between 2,800 to 6,000 people, depending on the source.[7] In the wake of the cruelty, the Saigon government felt comfortable declaring a complete mobilization— something they had avoided for fear of public opposition.

The revised General Mobilization Law placed the country's Regional Forces, Popular Forces (militias), and National Police Forces under the direct control of the South Vietnamese Army. The ranks of South Vietnamese forces swelled from 600,000 to 1,100,000. Back home, the increase gave Congress the perception that Nixon's policy of Vietnamization was working, and they approved funding for him to finish the job. Change was in the air throughout the first year of Nixon's presidency.

The Change that Trickled Down to My Hometown

That first summer I spent away from home was transformative. For the first time, I had an opportunity to explore the real world. Working with Roger Underwood, I made significant strides toward maturity, and stepping out of my comfort zone enhanced my perspective. As they say, travel encompasses more than simply reaching a destination; it fosters personal growth, worldly awareness, and expanded possibilities. As Roger taught me, each new stage in life brings new goals and callings to pursue.

I also felt strange when I returned to Smithville; it suddenly felt like I didn't "fit in" the way I used to. The activities and places that previously interested me no longer did. That's part of life after high school; you suddenly realize you have less in common with your old friends than you thought. I looked around and noticed how many people still did the same things as always, but I had moved on. It finally sank in that my life had changed, and there was no going back. Smithville would always be my hometown... but it was never the same again.

Do you want to know what changed? I have an easy answer: me! I'd changed because *faithfully doing small things prepares you for more significant opportunities*. I no longer "fit" in Smithville because I'd been elsewhere and exposed myself to hard work that required rigorous attention to detail. I could never go back to being the boy I'd been. My future lay elsewhere, in places and with people far beyond the edge of town.

Lynn West

I'd only been home for a few weeks when we learned Lynn's helicopter was shot down in the Mekong Delta. The Army listed him and his crew as missing-in-action. My family launched an around-the-clock prayer vigil, joined by friends and church members across the community.

While awaiting the news about Lynn, my father reminded me that hard times are temporary, but values and convictions are permanent. In moments of crisis, our core beliefs and unwavering principles serve as our compass, guiding us through the storm. They anchor us and provide clarity when chaos surrounds us. Even as I'd learned to be faithful with doing small things, like working for Roger, I also had to be vigilant against external realities I could not control as they attempted to undermine my faith. Life would still throw curveballs at me, and I had to learn to handle them.

After a few days, the dreaded news came: Lynn and his crew of three, plus two passengers, perished in a fiery crash. They were struck by ground fire during the opening days of the Tet Offensive. Grief is overwhelming for anyone, but for a teenager still navigating the complexities of self-discovery and self-identity, it felt excruciating and brutal.

The death of my classmates at the beginning of the war had been my first encounter with grief. Although challenging, the experience taught me to face the reality of war, find ways to cope with it and move beyond the pain and heartbreak. But Lynn's death took the sorrow to a new level. I experienced a range of intense emotions, including confusion, frustration, and anger. Uncertain of how to handle the turbulence, I buried it; I remained stoic and never wept at his funeral. In even deeper places, I subtly began believing God had ignored my family's prayers to protect Lynn from harm. I had yet to come to grips with the truth. Even though I could trust God's sovereignty, I shouldn't have mistaken it for invincibility in Lynn's case.

The apostle James wrote that trials prove our faith and Lynn's loss exposed some of the "unproven" places in my heart. I observed my public claims of belief... and then saw my actions based on how I truly believed in the depths of my soul. You can talk all you want about Christian values like faith, hope, and love. But if your actions betray feelings of distrust, despair, and hatred, you may as well throw in the towel. As theologian Dallas Willard said, "People's behavior tells you what they really believe, 100 percent of the time."

I found myself at another crossroads. I could choose the path of despair and cynicism... or broaden and expand my understanding of God.

Lynn lived well for twenty-nine years on this earth and is an excellent example of a man who showcased his values by living them. He demonstrated how to apply those values to real-life situations. As a teenager, Lynn listened as my sounding board for new ideas and questions, always providing constructive feedback and direction when I drifted off course. When I was at odds with my parents, Lynn reminded me of their sacrifices and commitment to my future. And now, when I needed him most because my faith seemed at risk... somehow, I still had him, even though he was gone. A remarkable thing about heroes is that they still have significant influence long after they're gone.

I could imagine what Lynn would say if I shared with him that I'd begun to doubt God. I knew he would listen to what I told him, and (through his questions and perspective) he'd force me to *think* about what I said. Of all the things I treasure about my relationship with him,

I most appreciate how often he helped me think through the fog in my soul and find my footing when I felt out of balance. I wanted to be more like Lynn—wise, thoughtful, deliberate, and self-controlled. His death, it turned out, was my first chance to follow through on that desire. He deserved the best response I could give in return for everything he'd given me.

Young Men's Burdens

At the age of eighteen, I'd already experienced tremendous losses. That wasn't "new" in the grand scheme of history. Plenty of young men throughout history experienced losses. But it certainly felt new to me. In a way, whether your draft number got called or not, teenagers in the late 1960s got roped into the painful process of losing friends and family members and then dealing with the difficulty of living without people they loved.

They also did the bulk of fighting in Vietnam. One of the ironies of Vietnam was how boys eligible for the draft at eighteen could be soldiers (and combat veterans) before their twentieth birthdays. Some warriors in Vietnam were as young as sixteen or seventeen. Compared with wars before or since, it was abnormal for the burden of national security to rest so heavily on so many teenaged shoulders.

People who criticized American soldiers in Vietnam never stopped to consider that the bulk of them were mere teenagers. Most of them weren't prepared, emotionally or spiritually, for the realities of the battlefield. This made their bravery even more remarkable. At the risk of their own lives, they went up against a vicious enemy on their home turf. Their enemies knew the land intimately and enjoyed every advantage they could—many of which were guaranteed by weak, unresolved American leadership. The generation of Vietnamese warriors we faced had already battled to rid their country of foreign invaders for over a decade. In the hand-to-hand combat sense, it was not a fair fight: a bunch of naïve American teenagers versus a trained and experienced army of grown men steeped in communist indoctrination.

Our leaders never considered the impact combat would have on the country's youngest warriors. Were they completely ignorant or just self-serving and indifferent? We'll never truly know. But we do recognize that our Vietnam veterans rose above the mischaracterizations, misrepresentations, and indignities thrown at them during and after the war. They returned home and accomplished even more than they had abroad despite a country that largely abandoned their mission and peers at home who held them in contempt.

In subsequent conflicts, the Vietnam Generation proved more heroic than words can say. As modern U.S. troops boarded flights and ships for lengthy wars in Afghanistan and Iraq, local veteran associations took it upon themselves to staff air terminals and ports at all hours, night and day, including holidays... just to be present and serve the younger generation. Away from the cameras and press, in modest transit points many Americans don't know about, Vietnam veterans *showed up*... while protesters and the mass of citizens slept or went about their days. They gave handshakes and hugs, listening ears, prayers, and solidarity... and they eased the tension these young soldiers felt, even if just a little bit.

You Can't Hide Forever

I began to sense God calling me to follow Lynn's example, to embrace the warrior's path, fill the gap, and pick up where he left off. I didn't know what it would entail and wasn't sure whether I could rise to the challenge. But I learned from watching my parents that answering God's call requires courage and faith. The Bible has many stories of people who answered it and began their journeys, knowing His guidance and support were always available. Lynn's example left ripples like a skipping stone across the waters of my life. Its waves reverberate to this day—a legacy I didn't know I should look for.

When enough time passed, I found my feet again. I refused the enemy's bait to doubt the heart of God. Instead, as much as an eighteen-year-old could, I chose to trust Him with the lives of everyone I loved... as well as my own. He is, after all, Lord of all

Creation. If He didn't spare His own Son but gave Him up to be crucified on a cross… what business did I have thinking He would arrange a special exemption for me or anyone I loved?

With the pain of Lynn's death subsiding and boyhood in the rearview mirror, I set about building for my future. By this time, my dad was a well-established residential contractor in Smithville, building the single-family homes that became popular in the postwar boom. Working with Dad, I learned carpentry and practical skills that went a long way in helping me survive the harsh world of Vietnam. I felt more aware than ever that at work, I didn't simply swing hammers and cut 2x4s; I was learning to *work with other people*. At any job you take, working with others is the hardest part.

Now that I'd finally stopped daydreaming and learned to focus, I excelled at getting along with people and working in teams. I felt a huge relief to mature—to work with my hands alongside other men on meaningful projects that served my community. In fact, it felt more satisfying than any Sixties fad I ever fell for. I found a profound consolation from the turbulence of my high school years, working hard for an honest living in the hot Tennessee sun.

The Real Sixties Revolution

As a nation, America remained polarized about politics, race, morals, sexuality, and religion—along with anything else we could find to be polarized about. If people could find something to be outraged and offended over, we wanted to join the cause! My generation's favorite drug of choice was outrage, with marijuana and LSD running close in second and third places. (Does this sound familiar in today's world?)

Amid the shrill voices and rhetorical assaults against traditional values, a genuine reform sprung up: the Jesus Movement. This evangelical Christian awakening began on the West Coast of the U.S. in the late Sixties and early Seventies. It spread like wildfire throughout the Western World and Central America.[8] Just as I had found a deeper level of peace and joy internally, many members of my generation began to "come home" to Jesus, where they found the consolation they'd been looking for. It's incredible how much more freedom, joy, and tranquility are available in *reform* versus revolution.

On February 3, 1970, at Asbury College (now Asbury University) in Wilmore, Kentucky, a morning chapel service turned into 144 hours of unbroken revival, with intermittent "encores" for several weeks. The Asbury Revival was a mighty outpouring of spiritual renewal, and after five years of nonstop ideological assault from the secular left, the Kingdom of God finally had a movement of its own.[9]

Fifty years after the revival, Lionsgate Pictures released a theatrical movie, *The Jesus Revolution*, which told the stories of some of the young people who took part in the movement. Students attending Asbury on the fiftieth anniversary of the revival spontaneously stayed in Hughes Auditorium, following a regularly scheduled chapel service, to hold a special anniversary event to commemorate the revival. The Jesus Movement and the Asbury Revival answered the spiritual hunger of young people—from strait-laced students to scruffy hippies.[10]

The Rendezvous with Destiny

As the flames of revival and spiritual renewal fanned out across the country, I felt their embers stir in my heart. Jesus' Parable of the Prodigal Son (see Luke 15:11-12) resonated most deeply with me. It's my story: like the prodigal son, I grew up with every advantage you could ask for, and it took me a long time to gain the wisdom and insight to appreciate it.

I was raised by Christian parents who loved me and, at every turn, sacrificed to give me opportunities to succeed. I was born into a prosperous and free postwar United States, where economic booms, widespread prosperity, and technological advances were the norm—expected, even. I was healthy, athletic, and surrounded by a good community. I had plenty of honest work with good pay. As Jesus often said, "To whom much is given, much is required." I took it all for granted and made a mess... but when I returned to my roots, my family and hometown were ready to receive me with open arms.

It was a good thing, too, because Uncle Sam sent me a "love letter" that summer. My draft number had been called.

Everything changed again once that letter arrived. My spiritual upbringing surged to life in July 1969, just two weeks before I was inducted into the U.S. Army. Until then, I'd been distracted by the humdrum of the counterculture, which left me spiritually depleted and unable to focus. But the draft notice pushed me to a crossroads in my relationship with the Lord and forced my hand. It was time to decide because I was about to risk my neck in a faraway jungle where many Americans died every day. You could say that summer, I gave myself *fully* to serving God, forever.

At every crossroads, the most crucial thing you can ask for is guidance. God offers it freely in moments like this. Looking back, I see how God used the people and events of the moment to guide me back home... just in time for the most significant and consequential season of my life. My parents, extended family, the local church, and community... suddenly, everyone I knew became a voice of prayer, encouragement, wisdom, and insight. It was as if there were some kind of divine conspiracy at work!

On Monday, August 11th, 1969, I said goodbye to my family and boarded a Greyhound bus bound for Nashville, the first stop on my journey to Vietnam. When we arrived, I felt nervous. I was eighteen, with little worldly experience. Yet there I was, at the Armed Forces Examining and Induction Center, where draftees gathered to undergo their pre-induction physical exam. After I passed, they sent me to Fort Campbell, Kentucky, for Basic Army Combat Training.

And so, my long and challenging journey began, leading me to where I am today. Tough lessons awaited me to prepare me for the challenges of war. Though I felt apprehensive, something about the process reminded me of what I already knew and had experienced in the past. Previously, I had ignored the call to manhood and leadership (with my parents) or had esteemed it too lightly (with Roger Underwood).

This time was different; I was resolute, even though it was intimidating. I could picture Lynn West smiling and applauding. For the first time, Larry Cripps stood his ground. The daydreaming, undisciplined boy from Smithville had changed and continued to change—I was mastering another stage of true manhood. I understood just enough to know that no matter what awaited in Vietnam, I would always have the *choice* of how to respond to it, just like I had with jogging for my parents, working for Roger, and responding to Lynn's death.

And as you already know, the Hope of War is what you make of it... and how you choose to respond to the circumstances life throws at you.

Chapter Seven
The Warrior's Crucible

Purpose **is more important than position. When goals and objectives seem unclear, switch gears and help others achieve theirs—until things change for you. God has a plan and a specific timetable for each person, individually ... and He also has a "general" plan for all of us, which consists of serving our fellow human beings.**

Days after the tragedy of September 11, 2001, members of an Army Special Forces team packed their bags, left their families, and headed for the ancient, faraway land of Afghanistan. While Americans at home struggled to accept what had happened, these men set out to strike the first blow of retaliation. They left with one goal: stop the enemy before he could strike again.

To protect the home front, the Green Berets had to reach the source of the attack without conventional military tactics by using an alternative strategy. The battlefront wasn't a traditional war, with militaries lined up and facing each other on opposite sides. Instead, they would have to combat the elements, ride horses over rough and dangerous terrain, and outwit opponents who knew the landscape like the back of their hand.[1]

Afghanistan's terrain and climate proved adversarial, even for the quiet insertion of a small team. Their helicopters had to approach the Hindu Kush Mountains at altitudes twice as high as they usually flew. Inclement weather kicked up, including sandstorms and black clouds of rain, snow, and ice. The enemy also sensed their approach and fired their weapons.

Captain Mark Nutsch led the twelve-man team into battle. Despite zero combat experience, his confidence and ability to think outside the box during the vetting process won him the assignment. Nutsch's experience growing up on his family's ranch, working as a ranch hand in college, and riding horses in rodeos proved essential to this particular mission.

The campaign should have taken six weeks, but due to a change in weather, they shrunk the timeline to three. The Army wanted to use multiple teams of Green Berets, but due to the elements, topography, and lack of entry points, they would have to manage with only one. Senior leaders anticipated casualties due to the risks, but every member of Nutsch's team came home in one piece. They knew how to adapt to the environment, unite local support, and employ unconventional methods (like riding horseback) to battle heavily armed enemies who often rode in tanks armed with missiles.

Though severely outnumbered, Nutsch and his team swelled their ranks quickly. They teamed up with Afghanistan's Northern Alliance and conducted constant assaults and raids on the Taliban, day and night, for three consecutive weeks. Perhaps Nutsch's lack of combat experience was, counterintuitively, best suited for the mission. His flexibility allowed him to approach it differently, leading to one of the quickest and most decisive victories in American history. The Green Berets and the Northern Alliance overthrew the Taliban and captured Mazar-e-Sharif, a strategic stronghold in Afghanistan. In 2018, Hollywood dramatized the adventure in the movie *12 Strong*, starring Chris Hemsworth.[2]

Nutsch and his team faced something every warrior must: *a crucible*—a trial by fire. U.S. Marines even refer to the final, most challenging phase of their Basic Combat Training (BCT) as "The Crucible." As raw ore is refined in intense heat to become steel, character, and resilience are forged through adversity. Crucibles temper our spirits, harden our resolve, and test our mettle at the core. They teach us to withstand pressure, adapt swiftly, and accept responsibility. When we pass through them, the lessons we learn carry forward like fires that stay lit forever.

Most of all, crucibles teach us the centrality of working *together*.

Two Steps Forward, Three Steps Back

President Richard Nixon faced a crucible prosecuting the Vietnam War that defined his legacy and influenced warfighting through to the present day. During the 1968 presidential campaign, he promised to end the war, secure the return of American prisoners of war (POWs), and establish a framework for peace. But once sworn in, Nixon came face-to-face with harsh realities.

Shortly after taking office, Nixon and his national security adviser, Henry A. Kissinger, conceded that the United States could not win a military victory in Vietnam. However, both believed the war could end with an honorable settlement that kept South Vietnam free from communist rule. Nixon argued that hasty American withdrawal would undermine our credibility worldwide. To achieve his envisioned settlement, Nixon planned to pressure the Soviet Union and China, who secretly desired to improve their relationship with the United States at the time.

The president decided to use direct force against North Vietnam, something Lyndon Johnson refused to consider for fear of China's intervention. To show Hanoi he was willing to bring the war to their doorsteps, Nixon greenlit General Creighton Abrams' strategy of bombing secret communist bases operating in neutral Cambodia near South Vietnam's border.[3] Cambodian leader Norodom Sihanouk, already tired of his (uninvited) North Vietnamese guests, agreed to the bombings within his country's borders. The North Vietnamese struggled to retaliate effectively against American aerial bombardment, and the Chinese retaliatory threat turned out to have passed its expiration date; Beijing sat on its promise to intervene.

So far, so good. Unless they wanted to reveal their violation of Cambodia's neutrality, North Vietnam could not complain about the Cambodian assault. Although the U.S. took elaborate measures to ensure the air attacks remained secret, the story nevertheless broke in *The New York Times* in May 1969. Infuriated by this security breach,

Nixon began a series of measures to plug "leaks" of information. These became part of a system of illegal surveillance and burglary known as "Nixon's Plumbers," which eventually led to the Watergate Scandal.[4]

The crucible's temperature kicked up a notch.

Between the performance of South Vietnamese armed forces during the Tet Offensive and public pressure to withdraw U.S. troops, Nixon ordered Abrams to accelerate Vietnamization. The U.S. provided South Vietnam with the weaponry and training needed to assume responsibility for the ground war. In June, Nixon announced the first withdrawal of 25,000 U.S. troops. Later, in September, he announced a phased withdrawal of 150,000 troops by the end of 1970.

This increased the temperature of Nixon's crucible by another few degrees; in a rush to quell the ongoing public outrage, he caved to publicly broadcasting parts of his strategy so the enemy could hear it. For the communists, this was helpful; they now had a timetable to wait until the U.S. completely abandoned South Vietnam.

The troop withdrawals placed Abrams between a rock and a hard place. He knew it was unrealistic to assume South Vietnamese forces could take on the bulk of the fighting at such a rapid pace. Moreover, the North Vietnamese would only commit to serious peace negotiations under pressure from the U.S.; they had little fear of facing the South Vietnamese themselves. Abrams had to find ways to navigate this delicate balance, which required doing more with fewer resources. Inevitably, tension spiked between the president and the commanding general.

For Nixon, this meant the crucible's temperature rose—by another several degrees. When a president overrules the better judgment of military commanders, he assumes personal responsibility for directing the war. That was a mistake Johnson had already made.

Though popular at home, in Vietnam, Nixon's decisions adversely impacted troop morale. They underscored the apparent pointlessness of the war: had it all been for nothing from the get-go? A severe drop in resolve followed among the rank-and-file. Drug abuse spiked, frequent and severe racial quarrels erupted, and some soldiers participated in "fraggings"—murder or deliberate maiming of officers using fragmentation weapons, such as hand grenades. Elsewhere, news of the My Lai Massacre, a mass murder of several hundred civilians by U.S. soldiers in Quang Ngai province, became public at the end of 1969. Perception, courage, and conviction about the war continued to plummet.[5]

Inside the crucible, things grew hot. Nixon was now alienated from many of his own staff, under siege from media controversy over Cambodia and My Lai, publicly sharing withdrawal plans with the enemy, at odds with military generals, and the soldiers under his command fell down spirals of cynicism, nihilism, and outright hostility toward each other.

While Vietnamization and troop withdrawals proceeded, the Paris Peace Accords remained deadlocked. Kissinger secretly opened talks with high-level North Vietnamese diplomats, but the two sides remained polarized. The U.S. proposed a mutual withdrawal of all forces. Hanoi countered and insisted on unconditional U.S. withdrawal and a neutral coalition government to replace the regime of Nguyen Van Thieu.

Increasingly isolated, Nixon pondered a renewed bombing campaign and a blockade of the North to coerce them back to the table. However, his military and intelligence experts advised against it, while his political advisers worried about the reactions of an American public eager to see the end of the war.[6]

The public would not see the end of the war that year. Or the next. Or for another three years afterward.

As for Nixon's crucible... it never cooled down, either. To compound his difficulties, the stalemate in Paris meant the bombing and fighting continued, and no one would feel better about it anytime soon.

My First Crucible

Nashville's Armed Forces Entrance and Examination Center was full of young men from every city, town, and community across the state of Tennessee. Because of its proximity to Fort Campbell, Kentucky, Nashville was the first stop in determining a draftee's physical eligibility for military service.[7]

The draft board classified me as "1A," which designated me as immediately available for military service. I joined a group of about twenty others awaiting instructions. A Marine recruiter entered the room and informed us of their search for volunteers because the Marines had fallen short of their enlistment goals that month. When nobody raised their hand to volunteer, I thought to myself, "Hmm... Marines are being killed in Vietnam faster than they can replace them!"

Then the recruiter said, "Okay, we'll do it the democratic way." He handed us a piece of paper with the names of all the branches of military service and told us to list our preferences from first to last. I put the Marines last. As we wrote on our papers, the recruiter reminded us, "No matter what, the needs of the service always come first." (I would hear *that* phrase many times throughout my military career, as most warriors do.)

In other words, this exercise was futile; if they decided to send us to the Marines, we didn't really have a say in the matter. The recruiter gathered our papers and walked out, leaving us sitting on edge for a while. When he returned, all but four people in the room got assigned to the Marines. I remained among the lucky four, seated next to another guy who also escaped the assignment. I told him, "We just escaped certain death by the skin of our teeth!"

After clearing medical exams and taking the Oath of Enlistment, we boarded Greyhound buses for a forty-five-minute ride to Fort Campbell. At the reception center, as we hurried off the buses and into formations, a cadre of Drill Instructors (DIs) in heavily starched olive drab fatigues barked orders laced with some of the most profane language I'd ever heard.

Hurry Up and Wait

We spent the rest of the evening filling out paperwork, under constant harassment and verbal assault for the slightest errors or infractions. The abuse is designed to humiliate and intimidate recruits into submission... and it works! I remember two muscular Iowa farm boys giving the DIs significant pushback, refusing to yield any ground to their intimidation. Their efforts didn't last long.

In-processing continued into the wee hours of the morning. We divided into several large groups, mixing with other young men who had arrived from various places throughout the country. Then, we boarded buses for the short ride to our temporary home—a set of World War II vintage wooden barracks. We stood in line for linens and rushed to find a bunk in the barracks. Most of us were so exhausted that we didn't bother making our beds; we simply fell asleep on our sheets.

The next three days consisted of aptitude tests, classification interviews (for Army jobs you qualified for based on your test results), post-test interviews (for jobs the Army needed to fill regardless of your scores), and dental and eye exams. Those who scored high on their aptitude tests could attend Officer Candidate School or the Enlisted Non-Commissioned Officer (NCO) Academy, better known as "Shake and Bake" school. However, both schools required a three-year enlistment contract versus a two-year draft commitment, so most of us declined.

I made friends with Jerome Phelps, a lightweight boxer from the inner city of Chicago. He helped me adjust to my new surroundings. We were an unlikely mix—a black man from the inner city and a small-town Tennessee farm boy. However, our friendship revolved around our mutual love of sports, and both of us grew up under strong Christian influence. Jerome was a soft-spoken yet powerful man with broad shoulders and narrow hips. Physically, he looked like a poster boy for Army recruiting.

Jerome's grandmother helped forge his gentle but courageous spirit, and her Christian example influenced his manner and worldview. We processed through the reception center together, and then I never saw him again. I later heard that one of the DIs bullied Jerome into a boxing match. After several weeks of harassment, he finally relented. The fight was over as soon as it started; Jerome knocked the man out with two punches.

With in-processing complete, we boarded a bus for the short ride to Army Basic Combat Training. The clock on your Army contract didn't move until you reached your assigned training battalion. I was glad to clear each hurdle without being held back. That would have prolonged my stay at the reception center and could have added time to my draft commitment.

As the bus made its way to the training areas, we passed row after row of uniformed white barracks—remnants of America's previous wars. These wood-framed structures became our home for the next eight weeks.

Day Zero and Beyond

Upon arrival, the DIs greeted us in typical Army fashion—loud, obnoxious, full of profanity, and in your face. They hounded us off the buses, screaming at full volume directly in our faces. If you've seen the basic training scenes from the Stanley Kubrick movie *Full Metal Jacket*, it's pretty accurate. The time had come for us recruits to train and think as part of a unit rather than as individuals. That kind of cohesion doesn't grow by itself. It requires *pressure*.

The DIs divided us into four large platoons (40-50 men) that comprised Delta Company, one of four companies (150-200 men) that belonged to the 6th Battalion, 2nd Training Brigade. From that day forward, we were no longer individuals but a group with a number: "Delta-6-2." This number became our brand, setting us apart from other companies in the brigade. It served as our "call sign," and we yelled it out at the beginning of every assembly or competitive gathering.

Fort Campbell was an enormous military base where soldiers trained and worked from dawn to dusk. It had barracks as far as the eye could see, representing previous generations of soldiers who served there. Delta Company had several facilities—an administration building, dining hall, game room, armory, and supply room. Roughly 150 to two hundred trainees made up each company, alongside twenty-five to thirty full-time staff members supporting them.

Delta's company commander, Captain Hubert T. Jacobs, was a seasoned infantry officer who had just returned from his second tour of duty in Vietnam. When the DIs presented us to him, Jacobs climbed onto a three-step platform in front of the orderly room to address us. His introductory speech made clear his stature as a formidable soldier, someone you didn't want to mess with.

We noticed his impeccable apparel. He wore a heavily starched tan khaki uniform adorned with infantry-related ribbons and accessories, highly polished black Corcoran jump boots, and a shining black and gold helmet liner. Adding to his appearance, he sported gold-framed aviator sunglasses, giving an air of pride and elegance. His appearance sent a subtle message to each recruit: "You won't be a real soldier unless you emulate my example." We understood the message loud and clear!

King of the Drill

Although historians can trace drill sergeants back to the Revolutionary War, the services didn't create a formal role until 1964, just before the Vietnam War began. Traditionally, the Army relied on experienced NCOs to train troops at four training centers across the nation. However, the lack of professionalism and training expertise among many of these "crusty" NCOs resulted in poor quality of training and low morale. In September 1964, the Army established a Drill Sergeant Academy at Fort Leonard Wood, Missouri, to address this issue. The goal was to attract top NCOs to the program and differentiate them from their peers. Each drill sergeant receives a special "This We'll Defend" badge and the infamous "Smokey the Bear" hat.[8]

My drill instructor was Staff Sergeant Tyrone Jones, a young and stocky black man from Alabama who had served two tours of duty as an infantry soldier in Vietnam. He returned home with both kinds of combat decorations—the ones pinned to his uniform and the ones scarred into his flesh. One thing that set Sgt. Jones apart from other DIs was his conservative use of obscene language. He believed profanity reflected a poor vocabulary and the best soldiers could communicate without using it. At first, we thought he was joking, but soon, we realized he practiced what he preached.

I often referred to Sgt. Jones throughout my career as an example to motivate sailors and Marines in cultivating their language skills. It helps them project greater self-confidence as instructors and leaders. During basic training, the DIs played a critical role in setting the tone for recruits' military experience. The more self-control they showed over their language, the more they inspired us.

Becoming a Warrior

As the saying goes, the Army accomplishes more before 7:00 a.m. than most people do all day, and nowhere does this ring truer than in basic training. The process challenges and engages recruits by stripping away familiar comforts, instilling the Army's values and warrior ethos, and preparing them to strike first before the enemy does.

In the early weeks, we focused on physical fitness, marching, and understanding the Army's rank structure, chain of command, customs, and traditions. The day started at 4:00 a.m. with a three-mile formation run in combat boots. Then, we had thirty minutes to shave, shower, dress, and make our beds before marching to the mess hall for breakfast. The DIs micromanaged the tiniest details of our existence; everything was done step-by-step, in a precise, orderly fashion. We even ate meals on command! After breakfast, we cleaned and prepared our barracks for a daily inspection. The outcome determined the favorability ranking of the four training platoons. The leading platoon of the day got special privileges over the rest, which led to competition.

The training intensified each week. We learned day and nighttime land navigation, fired at the rifle range, went through the dreaded gas chamber, threw hand grenades, and low-crawled through the nighttime live fire exercise. The low crawl lasted the length of a football field under a canopy of live M-60 machine gun fire while simulated artillery and mortar rounds exploded around us. We practiced the exercise several times during the day; at nightfall, we did it for real. It was an unsettling experience, requiring intense concentration and emotional fortitude, but it exposed us to some of the realities of actual combat.

During the final phase of training, a panel of DIs from a sister company evaluated us. Recruits who demonstrated progress in all major categories, such as general military knowledge, physical fitness, drill and ceremony, combat skills, first aid, marksmanship, and small unit leadership, usually got promoted by one pay grade at graduation. Delta Company received the top training award for its cycle, a testament to the commitment and capabilities of our DIs.

Our Senior Drill Instructor, Sergeant First Class (SFC) Tom Sanders, played a big role in our success. Sgt. Sanders served two tours of duty in Vietnam as an infantryman, first as a squad leader (in charge of 3-5 men) and then as a platoon sergeant (15-20 men). His heroics as a legendary airborne trooper on the battlefield propelled him ahead of his peers. Sanders stood as the central force behind Delta Company. He kept less-experienced DIs in check when they crossed the "fine line" between training and overplaying their roles. In a "company" (80-100 men), the first sergeant wears the highest enlisted rank. But in Delta-6-2, Sgt. Sanders held the most sway. Captain Jacobs deferred to him to ensure the safety and success of the unit.

During the final two weeks of training, the entire 2nd Training Brigade assembled at the post football stadium to hear from representatives from the Army's 101st and 82nd Airborne Divisions. After a hyped-up presentation highlighting the history, glory, and advantages of becoming an airborne paratrooper, they invited us to volunteer. Recruits filed out of the bleachers in droves to sign up for airborne training, but Sgt. Sanders moved up and down our section of bleachers, telling us to sit tight and reminding us that those who volunteered were headed for the infantry. I thought this strange then, considering Sanders served as a veteran infantryman. In hindsight, I believe he foresaw changes in the wind in Vietnam under the new administration. He knew our best chance of surviving the war was avoiding the infantry. As a result, only a few people from Delta Company stepped forward that day.

A Moment That Lasts Forever

Every Friday at Fort Campbell, a transformative ceremony took place where young recruits graduated as soldiers. A week before I graduated from basic training, Delta Company was tasked to set up the parade field for the weekly ceremony. Later, we welcomed family members, friends, and special guests to bear witness to the results of eight weeks of Army combat training. The transformation from civilian to soldier was amazing! Where a mix of skinny (or overweight) boys once stood, they now saw confident, slim, and physically fit young men—who had become soldiers to boot. Thanks to the commitment of our DIs and the rigorous training, we were ready for war. A group of soldiers that previously did not exist... now existed. I've learned once you bear that mantle, it never goes away as long as you live.

Pride and excitement filled the air as my battalion took the field the following Friday morning. The Army band's traditional military ballads and the precision formations of newly minted soldiers in their Army Class A uniforms brought it to a fever pitch. The audience stood in honor as the colors (flags) for the U.S., the Army, and each unit flapped in the wind ahead of each column. It's difficult to describe how it felt personally as a graduate. The DIs stopped screaming and abusing us, and they spoke to us as fellow soldiers. We were no longer recruits; we were *soldiers*.

Early in the training cycle, I focused on the bare minimum. I was unhappy about the sudden disruption of my life, and I lacked motivation. But my perspective changed when I remembered, as a Christian, that my goal was to first please God. I decided to become the best soldier I could, and I gave it everything I had, just like I'd learned to do for Roger Underwood. In the context of military service, that means that you serve God by serving your fellow soldiers. You give your last full measure of devotion to the people on your right and left—and you keep doing it, day after day until the crucible cools down and releases you with a new imprint of lessons you never forget.

Somewhere during that ceremony, the importance of being part of something greater than myself finally clicked for me. I'd become a member of a brotherhood and a tradition guided by bravery, loyalty, and selfless principles. The Army Creed passed down from generations of warriors, promotes values like teamwork, resilience, and honor. Over eight weeks, I learned the significance of cooperation and the power of working together towards a common goal. It transformed my thinking and gave me a sense of fulfillment. For me, graduation marked a significant rite of passage into the next phase of a meaningful and rewarding way of life.

The Lessons of the Crucible

The crucible shows you how far you have to go, if you insist on doing the job alone. I don't mean it shows "how awful, pathetic and powerless" you are. Instead, it challenges your assumptions that you can skate past responsibility, take care of yourself, or achieve success through sheer, individual willpower. You learn instead to rely on others and let them depend on you.

During basic training, the DIs hurled verbal abuse and drained us, physically and spiritually, from 4:00 a.m. to 10:00 p.m. (and sometimes later), seven days a week. But with each passing week, it subsided a little—especially as we stopped clinging to our individualism and learned to work as a team. We grew accustomed to the pace, standards and expectations, and our responses grew faster, while we made fewer and fewer errors. We took on the role of holding each other accountable rather than waiting for the DIs to notice a mistake.

The crucible also shows you what you *can* achieve as an individual… when you operate as part of a team! The military celebrates and recognizes individual achievement, but most of the time, it honors achievements from individuals who build, inspire, and fortify the team. If you pay attention to military award ceremonies, the common refrain is how the individual's achievement "reflects great credit upon themselves, their unit, the Army, and their country." The script uses those words for a reason; they remind us that we're at our best when we help *everyone* around us win.

Eventually, the pageantry of our graduation ceremony gave way to leeches, sweat, shrapnel, and the smell of napalm in the humid jungles of Vietnam. More recently, they gave way to burning sands, suffocating heat, camel spiders, dusty mountain ranges, and haunting calls to prayer in the darkness from Middle Eastern mosques. You go through one crucible so that you can go through another. The shiny moments between crucibles exist so you can recognize what you accomplish... but they never replace the accomplishments themselves.

Crucibles, in other words, eventually lead to *other* crucibles. We can't get around that. But if we want to survive them, the only way to do so is *together*. To go successfully from one crucible to another, we must learn to rely on others—and to be reliable for them—long after the shine of the dress uniform and the adulation of the crowd wear off. If I survived basic training by relying on my fellow recruits, I would have to survive Vietnam the same way.

I never forgot those lessons. They served me well... and they, too, are part of the Hope of War.

During the initial four weeks of basic training, we were not allowed to see anyone from outside. After Week Four, we could finally have two-hour visits with our loved ones. This photograph of me with my mother is from my family's first visit to see me at an area near Fort Campbell. Family photo.

Recruits arrive at the Army Reception Center in Fort Campbell, KY. Army basic training provided recruits with the skills and training necessary to become successful soldiers. The sign at the entrance is an iconic symbol of their journey towards becoming part of the U.S. Army. Photo adapted from public domain.

Chapter Eight
Good Morning, Vietnam

**A positive attitude comes more readily when life is going well,
but staying optimistic and faithful in difficult
or overwhelming circumstances becomes more difficult.
To be "bigger on the inside than the outside"
means your attitude transcends your circumstances.[1]**

President Richard Nixon believed an honorable end to America's involvement in the Vietnam War was paramount to the success of his administration. Amid widespread political and public discontent, the president estimated he had, at best, a year to help stabilize the situation in South Vietnam before troop withdrawals could begin.

Significant political and economic hurdles stood in the way of Nixon's Vietnam policy. He took office alongside the 91st Congress (1969-1971), where opposition Democrats held majorities in the House and the Senate. From the outset of the legislative session, lawmakers faced widespread problems on top of an unpopular war. Costly social programs carried over from the Lyndon Johnson administration and unlimited war spending triggered the first U.S. economic recession since the end of World War Two.[2] Major cities across the country convulsed under racial unrest, class disputes, and increasingly violent anti-war protests. Crime rose substantially, inflation continued to climb, and Soviet aggression worldwide showed no signs of slowing down.

The Democratic majority argued that the resources available to address home front issues were insufficient unless Nixon reversed course on America's foreign policy front. Congress set about the business of reducing military spending, curtailing U.S. commitments abroad, and forcing the debate on ending America's involvement in the Vietnam War.[3]

Overcoming the deck of cards history dealt to Nixon required resilience and endurance. For the first several years, he handled the situation surprisingly well. The president had confidence in his vast foreign relations experience, political grit, and willingness to pressure North Vietnam. He was convinced his strategy would yield the outcomes promised during his presidential campaign.[4] To achieve it, however, Nixon required the support of an ocean of voices that spoke louder than Congress, the anti-war movement, the media, or the Communist Party. He needed the American public to speak for themselves.

Setting the Stage

North Vietnam used the public peace talks in Paris as propaganda theater. They'd been "trained" for several previous years to make light of American diplomacy, whether it was benign or hawkish. Nixon concluded that productive negotiations could only take place in secrecy. He directed Henry Kissinger, his chief national security advisor, to arrange private talks with the North Vietnamese leader, Le Duc Tho. From now on, the secret Paris Peace Accords would keep the enemy off-balance and less confident of U.S. intentions or strategy.

During their first meeting in February at a villa outside Paris, Le stood firm. He insisted on the unconditional withdrawal of all U.S. troops on a fixed date—along with abandoning the South Vietnamese government—as preconditions for a settlement. North Vietnam had zero interest in Kissinger's proposals for mutual withdrawal of forces, neutralization of Cambodia, or mixed electoral commissions to supervise elections in South Vietnam. Two meetings followed, one in March and another in April 1970, but agreement remained elusive.[5]

Disappointed with the lack of progress, Nixon ordered a planning session to discuss strong-arming North Vietnam into peace negotiations. This political-military planning cell included members from the National Security Council, the Joint Chiefs of Staff, and MAVC staff officers in Saigon. In the end, Nixon concluded that no clear-cut political-military solution would end fighting as quickly as everyone hoped.[6] It would take time… and probably more casualties on both sides.

Rallying the Audience That Mattered

A year after his election, Nixon took to the airwaves and delivered his legendary "Silent Majority" speech to rally the American public. In it, he detailed his dual Vietnamization and negotiation strategy. The president explained why the further withdrawal of American troops would be disastrous for everyone concerned. He emphasized how the U.S. could not remain a great nation if we deserted our allies. Doing so would place the entire Pacific Theater in danger. In closing, Nixon emphasized, "In the previous administration, we Americanized the war in Vietnam. In this administration, we are Vietnamizing the search for peace."[7]

Nixon explained how America became involved in Vietnam. First, he reminded us that Americans are naturally do-it-yourself people who dislike waiting for someone else to do a job we can do ourselves. That resonated with the public, mainly when Nixon explained how this trait carried over into America's foreign policy. In postwar Europe, for example, and Korea, the United States furnished most of the money, arms, and men to help those countries rebuild and defend themselves against communist aggression.

Nixon believed the United States faced a choice in Vietnam between an immediate withdrawal of American military forces, regardless of the impact on the South Vietnamese people, or staying in the conflict until an honorable settlement could be reached. The latter meant withdrawing American military forces on a staggered basis, giving the South Vietnamese military time to prove strong enough to stand against North Vietnam.[8] It was a call for resilience and endurance.

Nixon's argument for prolonging the war was compelling. America's defeat and humiliation in South Vietnam would undoubtedly promote recklessness among the councils of "the great powers who have not yet abandoned their goal of world conquest," as Nixon described them. It would encourage violence wherever we had commitments to maintain peace, such as in the Middle East, Europe, and the Western Hemisphere. It would bring *more* war rather than less and cost more American lives. For these reasons, Nixon rejected the cry to end the war immediately. Instead, U.S. policy on negotiations and on the battlefront needed to change.[9]

Nixon took a genuine and masterful approach to his speech. He connected with the American people and helped them understand their frustration and discontent over the war. From the people's perspective, there had been no precise "end state" in Vietnam, and casualties had continued to mount with each passing day. More than 30,000 Americans had lost their lives in Vietnam at this point, and the "light at the end of the tunnel" seemed no closer now than at any other time. The people needed reassurance that the country was headed in the right direction.

That Was Then, This Is Now

Yet, there also occurred a shift: the U.S. could not continue fighting for South Vietnam as it had for Europe and Korea. Henceforth, when assisting other nations in protecting their freedom, U.S. policy had to evolve to help other countries fight their wars... without fighting the wars for them.[10] Though Nixon did not waste words blaming his predecessors for this, his acknowledgment represented a turning point. The protracted, undefined, and endless nature of the Vietnam conflict had already sacrificed a great degree of U.S. credibility and respect on the world stage. We could not hope to recover it soon; the post-World War Two "American Century" bloom was, in some ways, off the rose.

Nixon outlined three guiding principles to move forward. First, he reaffirmed U.S. commitments to treaties. He promised a defense shield in case a nuclear power like the Soviet Union threatened U.S. allies or strategic interests. The U.S. would provide military and economic assistance under our treaty commitments when requested. And, in going forward, America would no longer assume the primary responsibility of defending other nations from communist aggression. "The defense of freedom," Nixon emphasized, "is *everybody's* business—not just the United States."

When the Wicked Tremble

Nixon's speech terrified North Vietnamese leaders. They read between the lines and took seriously his threat of expanding the war to Hanoi's doorsteps. They'd hoped, with all the continued public outrage over bombings in Cambodia and Laos, that he would make concessions to appease the domestic anti-war movement. Instead, the speech did the opposite. It rallied the American public, encouraged the president, and for the first time in five years of fighting, North Vietnam felt themselves at a political disadvantage.[11]

Hanoi issued a counterstatement, hoping domestic U.S. opposition would surge. They characterized Nixon's speech as "intimidating, arrogant, and war-like." They predicted adverse editorial and congressional reactions to Nixon's speech, which would interfere with the president's agenda. They got their wishes to some extent—but it wasn't enough to overcome the groundswell of support Nixon received from the Silent Majority.

Dividing Enemies Against Themselves

Nixon gave North Vietnam even more reason to panic when, in 1972, he became the first U.S. president to visit the People's Republic of China—the behemoth communist nation of 750 million people that, next to the Soviet Union, was America's fiercest adversary in the Cold War.[12] While Johnson spent most of his presidency directing the Vietnam War to *avoid* upsetting China, Nixon took advantage of deteriorated relations between China and the Soviets to splinter their communist solidarity. Effectively, this backed North Vietnam into a corner; if China's support was compromised by diplomacy and greater cooperation with the U.S., North Vietnam's bargaining posture shrank considerably.

Buoyed by unity and support from the American electorate, Nixon signaled North Vietnam that they would have to keep fighting. There would be no reprieve, no ceasefire, no fixed timetable for the withdrawal of U.S. troops, and no further announcements regarding withdrawals beyond the 60,000 scheduled for December of 1969.[13]

A Gallup Poll survey after the speech indicated that seventy-seven percent of Americans trusted Nixon. Congress reacted favorably as well; although prominent Democrats, like Senator J. William Fulbright of Arkansas, questioned Nixon's sincerity, more than three hundred members of Congress and forty senators co-sponsored resolutions supporting the president's agenda.[14]

Running a Race of My Own

Meanwhile, I reported to the Army Aviation Center at Fort Rucker (known today as "Fort Novosel"), Alabama, in November 1969 for Advanced Individual Training (AIT). After Basic Combat Training, AIT is the second step in a soldier's preparation for duty. In those days, you didn't get to "choose" your Military Occupational Specialty (MOS) the way modern soldiers do. When I graduated from Basic Combat Training, I thought Providence had smiled on me. I avoided the infantry and drew an MOS in aviation logistics and motor transport.

During the Vietnam Era, Rucker hosted the final phase of Army helicopter pilot flight training and numerous tenant commands responsible for conducting AIT. Aircraft mechanics, helicopter crew chiefs, door gunners, and anyone associated with helicopter operations underwent Military Occupation Specialty (MOS) training at Fort Rucker.

Learning the Ropes

Here's one thing you get used to in military life: *uncertainty*. It takes time to accept and fully adapt to the lifestyle. I didn't yet understand how many "variables" the military imposes on the individual warrior. I had even less awareness of how much I had to learn about resilience and endurance. You might picture *physical* endurance as someone running a marathon... but the most challenging kind of endurance is spiritual. When everything around you constantly changes, and nothing "resolves," it's exhausting. Many people reach a breaking point and run away or give up.

But other things were more certain. One of them was training. I learned everything possible about military transport vehicles—especially equipment used to load military aircraft. I worked with the Boeing CH-47 "Chinook" helicopter – a dual-rotor, heavy-lift aircraft used extensively throughout the Vietnam War to transport and resupply ground forces. I managed cargo according to a helicopter's weight restrictions and rigged external loads, such as pallets of munitions, artillery pieces, water and fuel bladders, and anything else troops might require on the battlefield. Hardly a day went by without some kind of training!

I felt overwhelmed by the amount of knowledge I had to absorb, especially at such a pace. Our instructors kept us motivated by emphasizing the importance of dedication, focus, and adaptability. They taught us how critical split-second decisions could be if we had to make them in Vietnam. When seconds seem to take hours, soldiers must be ready in the heat of the moment and remember their training and knowledge. They repeated this over and over, leaving a deep impression on me and paying huge dividends later.

For two months, I immersed myself in learning manuals on weapons tactics, first aid, and land navigation. I honed my skills relentlessly, knowing people in Vietnam would depend on me for their lives. Thanks to my farming and construction experience, I quickly mastered the various transport vehicles and specialized equipment for my MOS. Hard work and commitment paid off as I stood out among my peers, raising the prospects of a job at Rucker after graduation. At this point, with Vietnam's changing political and military situations, I remained hopeful of avoiding the conflict altogether. A job at Rucker sounded like the perfect "escape" from duty in Southeast Asia.

Flying Below the Radar

But my hope didn't last. In late 1969, President Nixon altered the strategy and public perception of the Vietnam War. I had been hopeful his reassessment of the U.S. military's role would end fighting sooner or, at least, slow down troop deployment cycles. Instead, the people rallied toward Nixon's "peace with honor" agenda. The fight wasn't over yet, and the Vietnam Generation had several more sacrifices to make.

I graduated from AIT the following February. To my delight, the job at Rucker materialized, and they reassigned me to the base's Technical Support Company. I handled resident units' transportation and equipment needs, notably the Army's Advanced Helicopter Flight Training Center.

During the Vietnam War, helicopter pilots who flew the iconic Bell UH-1 "Huey" helicopters finished training at Rucker. The student pool included warrant officer candidates (mostly eighteen to nineteen years old with high school diplomas) and commissioned officers, ranging from complete novices to experienced combat leaders. After initial training at Fort Wolters, TX, graduates proceeded to Rucker for an additional four months of advanced flight and ground instruction.

Rucker trained over five hundred pilots every month, most of them in preparation for service in Vietnam. I worked at the Post Transportation Dispatch Office, supervised by Specialist 6th Class Jerome Powers (SP/6, an equivalent to today's rank of E-6 Staff Sergeant). He was one of my AIT instructors. During the Vietnam War, the Specialist ranks represented specialized expertise. SP/6 Powers was among the best when it came to transportation and equipment. He carried a lot of clout with leadership on base, and working for him was a good experience for me.

The student pilots did very well during their training, albeit not without accidents. Three fatal crashes occurred during my stint at Rucker. The first happened a few weeks after I started, and I volunteered to be the driver for the investigation team. The wrecked Huey had flown off-course, making it arduous to reach the crash site, but that wouldn't stop a Tennessee farm boy in a Jeep! From that time forward, investigative teams began asking for me by name.

When off-duty, I felt optimistic enough about remaining at Rucker to get involved in a local church. This allowed me to expand my network of friends and grow a support base, making life in the Army seem a little more like a regular civilian job.

Then word came suddenly: I received orders to Vietnam. It shattered my hopes of escaping the war; the vision of a smooth and pleasant journey through the Army vanished. I recall thinking, "Ah, the delightful dance of unexpected moments—so common in Army life!"

Expect the Unexpected

My father once warned me to "expect the unexpected" when serving in the military. I didn't understand what he meant then, but I found out when I checked out of Fort Rucker.

Checking out from Rucker involved a medical examination to ensure my fitness for duty in Vietnam. I had to undergo weapons re-familiarization training, a week-long field exercise. SP/6 Powers used his clout with the range officer to sign my rifle scorecard so I could skip the training, which (considering my destination) was both wrong and foolish. But I only cared about getting through the necessary hurdles to pick up my orders, pack my belongings, and head home on pre-deployment leave. In some ways, I remained very committed to my own agenda.

By skipping a week in the field, I out-processed quickly, which meant I could take leave to spend time with my family. I was thrilled to see my loved ones again and enjoy some trout fishing with Dad. Before heading home, I stopped by the personnel office to pick up my orders and sign out. It was midday; if everything went well, I could be back in Smithville by late evening.

The administrative clerk handed me my orders. When I read them, I noticed the unexpected change my father predicted. My MOS had been changed—from 64B2O (Vehicle Transport) to 67N2O (UH-1 Helicopter Repairman/Door Gunner). After I pointed out the mistake, the clerk shrugged and told me to file a grievance with the administrative chief, a crusty warrant officer named Jones.

When I told Warrant Jones about the mistake, he said, "The Army doesn't make mistakes." They made the change because they were short of people to fill aviation roles, and I was among those chosen to fill the gaps. Although I protested several times that I hadn't been trained as a helicopter door gunner, he said, "The Army will teach you what you need to know once you get to Vietnam. The needs of the Army come first." (There's that saying again.) The conversation ended. I signed the register, did an about-face, and exited the building, kicking anything in my way as I went.

My anger at the unexpected change hinted that I still had some growing up to do. I felt willing to take on challenges and endure difficulties to become the best version of myself, but I needed to change the phrase I silently attached to my willingness: "...as long as I'm in control." I wasn't in control, and this was God's way of showing me who truly pulled the strings.

Enduring the Spiritual Marathon

Remember how I said the enemy has plans for us, even if we're "one of the good guys"? I'd come a long way since that summer of 1967, working for my uncle. I felt as though I'd overcome a lot of self-imposed barriers. But it turned out I'd also taken on a few new delusions. One was a lack of true *submission*—surrendering all outcomes to God, including the ones I don't like. Submission is a balancing act somewhere on the spectrum between being a "control freak" versus being a nihilist. I'd learned to work my tail off to get what I wanted; now, I had to learn when to back off and let God lead me to where *He* wanted me to go.

Author Richard Foster defines submission as "the ability to lay down the terrible burden of needing to have our way." Previously, I'd been a fun-loving daydreamer who didn't care where he went. Now, I was a driven young man, seeking to get ahead and control my destiny, whatever it took. I believed I had the wit, strength, and determination to outwork others and get what I was after. I spent a lot of time trying to "make" things happen because I didn't understand God or how He worked. I spent my first few months of active duty fighting for a future when God had already planned one for me.

Would you agree that submission is a crucial component of endurance and resilience? Ask anyone who's ever worn a military uniform—changed orders, mission priorities, and even clerical errors upend the best-laid plans of mice and men. What can we do about it? I thought I'd secured an address on Easy Street at Fort Rucker, driving Jeeps over rough terrain, just like back on the farm in Smithville. The next thing you know, I'm on a flight to Southeast Asia to do a job I'd never trained for—one of the most dangerous in all the Vietnam War. Who wanted to submit to that?!

I was a poor "submitter"—no doubt about it. I lived as a subject of the Kingdom of God who still thought he existed in a democracy rather than a monarchy. I needed to learn what it meant to depend on

God instead of my wit and instincts. Mother Teresa once said, "You will never know God is all you need until He is all you have." God knows we're most likely to turn to Him when we run out of options... so He removes the options! We interpret moments like these negatively, like we're being "sold down the river" or abandoned. But God isn't confined by these challenges as we are. He sees them for their true purpose: opportunities to grow our faith.

Lynn West's death, along with the three helicopter crashes at Rucker, was enough to convince me that serving aboard Huey helicopters in Vietnam was a dangerous business. But God planned for me to embrace my purpose and lose myself in walking it out. If His plan meant serving as a door gunner on a Huey in Vietnam, I had to trust Him to take complete responsibility for my life. Even if it meant that, for me and my journey, Vietnam was "the end of the line."

Military life has an abundance of frustrating, unexpected turns and twists. We can only truly control how we respond to them. We can let fear take over or approach situations with curiosity and an open heart. How we think about and interpret our lives plays crucial roles in shaping our resilience and endurance. It's like trying to dance when a band plays out of sync and off-key; most people plug their ears and stop dancing. But the children of God must keep dancing with courage and vulnerability, even when the soundtrack falters, the singer hits the wrong notes, and the rhythm is out of place.

Saying goodbye to my family at the airport in Nashville was an emotional, heart-wrenching experience. Combat deployments create enormous challenges for families to handle. They live in constant tension and suspense, never knowing if they might be the next recipient of a message, beginning with the words, "We regret to inform you..." Family members battle media reports, rumor mills, caring for young children, and the bureaucratic complexities of military family life. Especially during Vietnam, the lack of public support and strategy from leadership made saying goodbye very difficult and painful for many family members.

Fortunate Son

On my flight from Nashville to the Army Overseas Replacement Center in Oakland, California, I had time to reflect on the events leading up to my departure. The days before leaving home were filled with final tasks and occasional tears. Reflecting on all this, I remembered a poem by the celebrated Chinese poet Li Po around 750 A.D. In the poem, Li expressed his disdain for the brutality and futility of war:

> *"Men are scattered and smeared over the grass, and the generals have accomplished nothing."*[15]

The vivid imagery evoked a sense of desolation and loss from war. Many men died, and many generals in Vietnam accomplished little. Was this how it would end for me as well? Would I spend my last days fighting a meaningless, unwinnable war in a faraway jungle? Why had God singled me out to serve on Hueys, like Lynn? What was the point of enduring all those terrible losses in Smithville, of so many families and friends, only to end up as another one of the casualties?

As President George Washington said, these are the times that try men's souls. The temptation was thick, like a black fog swirling through my mind, fighting tooth and nail to turn my heart against God. I dug deep, remembering the warning from Scripture that God "disciplines everyone He welcomes as a son." I had a root of pride and self-sufficiency that had to be removed, and God chose a Huey in Vietnam as the environment to teach me true submission and humility.

Checkmate.

Across the Pond

By the time we reached Oakland, I'd made up my mind: God had me right where He wanted me, no matter what it looked like. He *wanted* me on that gunship. He wanted me to trust Him in places and under circumstances where I had no clue what was going on, much less could I control the outcome. The best place for a guy like Larry Cripps to learn those lessons was "a hot LZ" (landing zone).

We flew from Travis Air Force Base near Oakland to Bien Hoa Airbase in South Vietnam. The journey included stopovers in Hawaii and the Philippines. For most Vietnam veterans, Bien Hoa was the "Start" and "Finish" line of their participation in the conflict. As we boarded our aircraft from the Philippines into Vietnam, several tanned soldiers returning from Vietnam disembarked from it. It was surreal; we boarded through the rear hatch while the returning veterans exited from the front. As the two groups passed each other, catcalls rang out, warning us about where we were headed.

When we landed, I was struck by the resilience of Vietnamese civilians moving about with little urgency despite the war-torn environment. The tropical heat and humidity slithered underneath our uniforms, bathing us in sweat in no time at all. Above the chatter of the terminal, someone let loose a full-throated shout: "Good morning, Vietnam!" (Yes, that was a thing before the movie featuring Robin Williams.) We'd reached the "point of no return" on a journey of discovering new levels of heroism, resilience, and endurance. Behind us lay everything we'd known and understood—a world we'd never truly return to.

Ahead lay the Hope of War.

Chapter Nine
The View of War from Quan Loi

Servant leaders surround themselves with the right influences and serve with integrity, even when no one is looking. This focus empowers them to influence people of various backgrounds, interests, and beliefs.

When the news broke in May 1970 that President Richard Nixon authorized secret bombings of communist bases in Cambodia (Operation *Menu*), congressional opponents of the war went berserk. After all, Secretary of State William Rogers had just testified before the Senate Foreign Relations Committee, claiming the administration had no plans for offensive operations beyond South Vietnam's borders. Rogers was unaware Nixon intentionally excluded him from the planning meetings to avoid leaks to the press that would alert North Vietnam of his intentions. Congress concluded that Rogers deliberately lied to their committee under the president's direction, which led to swift and heated outrage.[1]

In early 1970, MACV intelligence officials believed they had pinpointed the communists' political and military headquarters, known as the Central Office of South Vietnam (COSV), in Cambodia's "Fishhook" region. The Fishhook was part of Kampong Cham Province, located near the border with South Vietnam. It protruded like a fishhook into the Bihn Long and Tay Nihn provinces of South Vietnam. As one of the terminus points of the Ho Chi Minh Trail, this area was one of the most dangerous places in Southeast Asia. During the war, North Vietnamese and Viet Cong forces set up logistical bases and rest areas there.

General Creighton Abrams believed fighting the North Vietnamese in Cambodia could help force peace negotiations. Cutting off the enemy's entry point through Cambodia would prevent them from launching another war-altering maneuver, like the Tet Offensive. It would weaken their position politically and put them on the defensive.

Abrams also believed it would accelerate Vietnamization efforts and de-escalate the war. Then, at long last, U.S. forces could withdraw.

To support Abrams' strategy, Nixon made the controversial decision to extend the conflict beyond the borders of South Vietnam. On April 28, 1970, he ordered U.S. troops to invade communist "sanctuary bases" in Cambodia. He did not immediately announce it to the American public; instead, he waited two days before making a televised statement. Predictably, this incensed Congress, the media, and the anti-war establishment.

Hearts and Minds Divided

Hanoi enjoyed a distinct advantage over Washington in terms of their view of the war's parameters. The U.S. viewed Cambodia and Laos as impartial states; they simply couldn't conceive of how differently North Vietnam saw them. It was like wondering why the Nazis wanted to recapture Austria and the Sudetenland prior to World War Two. For the forces of darkness, history is only "written by the victors" when *they* win. North Vietnam perceived Laos and Cambodia the same way they did before the Geneva Accords, simply as other regions of one nation, as Tennesseans think about the states of Montana and New Hampshire. In the words of National Security Advisor Henry Kissinger, "Washington was convinced that the four Indochina states were separate entities, even though the communists treated them as a single theater for over two decades and were conducting a coordinated strategy in respect to them."[2]

Even as field commanders implemented Nixon's strategy and fought to keep American casualties at a minimum, U.S. lawmakers struggled to relate to the North Vietnamese mindset. Couldn't the Vietnamese read maps? To Western leaders, borders mark sovereignty as official lines to be respected, with proper crossings and customs enforcement. Congress could not fathom the communists' more lenient definitions, no matter how often field reports told them otherwise.

This situation turned Nixon's strategy from a promising path to a pointless, lengthy, academic debate over executive privilege and presidential war powers. Congress blamed Nixon instead of the North Vietnamese; they had little interest in the truth, which field commanders serving in Vietnam could easily have told them. The enemy had *zero* qualms about fighting dirty, violating international sovereignty, and sacrificing one life after another in pursuit of their cause. How could we expect to defeat them by insisting they fight fairly? It was like refusing to use the atomic bomb until the Japanese voluntarily abided by the Geneva Conventions. It wasn't going to happen!

At any rate, none of that mattered to Congress. They just wanted to quell the anti-war movement and the media (...which also wasn't going to happen). U.S. legislators already had their minds made up regarding which voices they planned to heed.

The Voices We Listen To

South Vietnam's president, Nguyen Van Thieu, offered little in the way of help. Although a staunch anticommunist, Thieu's focus was on staying in power regardless of the human and economic costs to his people. The South Vietnamese were unenthusiastic about his leadership and disagreed among themselves about the direction of their country. Thieu made the mistake of allowing South Vietnam to remain dependent on U.S. military and economic assistance—mainly, it turned out, for personal gain. This decision bound him to Washington's diplomatic choices regarding the "neutrality" of neighboring countries such as Cambodia and Laos. Like Congress, Thieu had already made up his mind about which voices he would consider.

As the story unfolded, everyone had their trusted sources. Thieu listened to Washington. Congress listened to the media and the antiwar movement. Nixon listened to his advisors. And Le Duc Tho, the North Vietnamese leader, listened to his supporters in Moscow and Beijing. There was only one group of people whose experience, opinions, and insight no one really cared to hear: *the American soldier*. What a pity; we could have told them plenty had they been willing to listen.

As an old saying goes, "The right voices lead to the right choices." Look among the best leaders in history, the ones everyone wishes they had, and you'll find they have this characteristic in common. Servant leaders recognize that they hold an office of tremendous impact and responsibility and avoid isolated decision-making like the plague. They carefully choose the voices they allow to influence their thinking, and if they've personally experienced the conditions and consequences their decisions create, it's a plus!

Come to think of it, political leaders of all stripes who oversaw the Vietnam conflict could have done with a tour of duty. Had it been up to me, I would have put them through the training I received at Camp Di An, my last stop on the way to the combat outpost at Quan Loi. In the final weeks before I entered combat, I witnessed some of the finest examples of servant leadership I've ever seen.

Into the Jungle

The 90th Replacement Battalion was the first stop for new arrivals entering South Vietnam through Bien Hoa Air Base. At this entry point, soldiers learned their assigned locations for the duration of their tour in Vietnam.

The staff didn't call for me on the first day, so I took a turn guarding the firebase's perimeter with a fellow soldier that night. We stood watch on a sandbag-constructed bunker, scanning for potential enemy infiltration. My companion claimed an enemy had breached the perimeter wire by our post and slit the throats of the men in the bunker. I figured he made the story up, hoping I would stay up all night while he slept. It worked; I didn't get one wink of sleep.

The next day, I received my orders to Headquarters and Headquarters Troop (HHT), 2nd Squadron, 11th Armored Cavalry Regiment, based at Camp Di An. I had never heard of them. I asked one of the staff, who told me, "Blackhorse troopers are always at the forefront of the fight. In fact, the 2nd Squadron is currently making news by leading the charge in Cambodia. I suspect you'll join them. Consider yourself fortunate, for there are no better warriors."

After three more days of anxious waiting, we finally headed for Camp Di An. When we arrived, we met the senior enlisted in charge of Squadron S-1 (Personnel). I scheduled a meeting with him to discuss the problem with my MOS and explained how I hadn't been trained to serve as a helicopter door gunner. He promised me he would discuss the situation with the troop commander.

Blackhorse Legacy

We met the squadron adjutant, who gave us an overview of the 11th Cavalry's mission and their expectations of us as soldiers. He said, "You're fortunate to wear the Blackhorse unit crest and shoulder patch. We expect you to exemplify the courage and the spirit of the legendary cavalry tradition. Doing anything less is entirely unacceptable." I remember thinking, "I hope I don't disappoint him."

We learned that Colonel George S. Patton III, the son of World War II General George S. Patton, Jr., had commanded the regiment the year before. Like his famous father, Colonel Patton had a reputation for thinking outside the box. He understood better than most of his peers that counterinsurgency warfare required imaginative thinking and risk-taking, well-known Patton family traits.

Colonel Donn A. Starry, who later became a four-star general, succeeded Patton. He, too, had a reputation for creativity in Vietnam. I once had the opportunity to meet Col. Starry and the squadron's command sergeant major (CSM), Master Sergeant Robert Bolan, who died later that summer when his helicopter was shot down. He had less than two weeks left in Vietnam and left behind a widow and three children. When he died, the entire regiment mourned his loss.

I later heard numerous stories about Master Sgt. Bolan and his ability to adapt cavalry and armor tactics to Vietnam's unforgiving terrain. This skill typically took platoon and squad leaders an entire tour to master, but Bolan seemed to have the instinct to size up a situation and adjust his movements quickly. He was renowned for his bravery during close-quartered encounters with the enemy. On one occasion, he single-handedly rescued several besieged troopers, earning a Silver Star and then, later on, two Bronze Star medals with the "V" device for valor.

The Training that Set the Tone

We reported to the Blackhorse Replacement Training Center, referred to by its cadre of instructors as "Blackhorse Dumbass School." Our instructors, noncommissioned officers in their early to mid-twenties, were a hard-core, experienced group of Blackhorse troopers—the cream of the crop. One of the instructors' favorite sayings was, "The Army expects us to transform chicken hawks into eagles, yet they keep sending us crows to work with."

We trained in landmines, booby-trap detection, and recognizing signals like colored smoke grenades. To test our knowledge, we walked a trail with a sign at the entrance that said, "Dead Walk! Do Not Enter Without a Guide." This trail had a variety of booby traps: some with trip wires attached to hand grenade simulators and others that included punji pits (sharpened stakes in a hole in the ground covered with leaves or grass). We spent two days on the rifle range, qualifying on our newly issued M-16s, followed by a course in laying and setting Claymore anti-personnel mines.

UH-1 Huey helicopters were an everyday part of life in Vietnam, so we trained to embark and disembark from them, emphasizing speed without sacrificing safety. The last training phase was the most challenging; it focused on night tactics, such as setting up an ambush or running a dismount (foot) patrol. During one part of the exercise, they blindfolded us to simulate an enemy nighttime ground assault. We had to locate and charge our M-16s, work the radio, and start the engine of our tracked vehicle—all while our instructors shouted out orders to cause confusion and simulate the chaos. It was excellent training that taught us to remain calm and focused while navigating the chaos of combat once on our job.

Serve Like Nobody's Watching... Because Someone Is

I've never forgotten those instructors. They gave exceptional training in a time and circumstance where they could have easily "checked the box" and left us unprepared for what lay ahead. Nobody looked over their shoulders; they could have been far more casual and cynical, going through the motions with one more group of trainees. Instead, they treated our survival as their solemn responsibility. They knew only too well the realities of war and its devastating consequences.

The instructors stood by their convictions, ignored all the hullabaloo back home, and focused on their mission. When you follow a purpose bigger than yourself, you stand out from the crowd. Other units who served alongside Blackhorse sometimes criticized us because of our so-called "swagger." They failed to recognize that behind the bluster lay *conviction*—to be the best at what we did, regardless of what others did. The fierce intentionality of our instructors set the tone for my entire tour, and the soldiers I served with in Quan Loi reinforced it.

Looking back, I clearly see that the last thing God wanted me to review before entering combat was *servant leadership*—and what great examples He provided! The Bible teaches that whatever we do, we must do it for the glory of God. This approach means that even if we don't face earthly consequences for our actions, we will most certainly face heavenly ones. But if we serve our fellow human beings with honor, even when no one's looking, we can know for sure that God sees and will generously reward us on that day when we stand before Him.

Before we left Camp Di An for Quan Loi, I received word regarding my MOS. I was safe for now since all the door gunner positions were filled. In the end, they never called on me to do the job. It was... "just a drill."

Welcome News

Another good piece of news was that my brother, Fred, didn't have to do a second nine-month tour of duty in Vietnam. The routine for Navy Seabees at the time was six months in their home port and then back to Vietnam. As a much smaller community than their counterpart in the Army, the Corps of Engineers, Seabees are always in high demand during wartime. They're also more specialized and tackle a wider range of projects, from road construction to infrastructure development.

Fred knew about the mix-up with my MOS and decided to leverage the situation to get a better deal. He told his section chief I was serving as an Army helicopter door gunner in Vietnam. Thus, under the military's Sole Survivor policy, that exempted him from returning to Vietnam. The sole survivor policy was a long-held tradition that protected families that had already lost, or were at risk of losing, their members in wartime. This same policy was central to the plot and titular character of the 1998 film *Saving Private Ryan*, starring Tom Hanks.

Although skeptical, Fred's section chief presented his argument to the battalion commanding officer for consideration. Within a few days, the Navy transferred Fred to the on-base student training command for the remainder of his time in the service.

Fred gave me some brotherly advice before I left for Vietnam, which stayed with me throughout my military career. He said, "When your integrity is tested, when the rest of the world begs you to be someone other than you are, be true to yourself and God, and glorify Him in whatever you do." For as long as I can remember, my older brother always had my best interests at heart. He expected a lot from me, which kept me from quitting when life grew difficult.

No Further Delays

The day finally came to board a ground convoy to Quan Loi, home to the 1st Cavalry Division (Airmobile) and the temporary command

and control center for three squadrons of the 11th Armored Cavalry Regiment. Quan Loi lies in a rugged region with occasional dense jungles, rolling hills, and numerous rivers and streams. Since the beginning of the Vietnam War, it was an infiltration point for North Vietnamese and Viet Cong forces—from Cambodia into South Vietnam.

The convoy had to travel up Highway 13, dubbed "Thunder Road" by Blackhorse troopers due to the number of landmines and ambushes the previous year. Once we assembled in the staging area, one of the instructors from Blackhorse Dumbass School showed up to see us off. He asked the convoy leader if he could brief the group since it was our first ride.

The instructor reminded us there were no "front lines" in Vietnam. The enemy often pounced when you least expected him, and he told us that we could plan on being observed by the Viet Cong throughout the trip. Because of their limited resources, the Viet Cong never attacked unless they felt confident they could win. They were constantly looking for ways to exploit weaknesses in our defenses. The only way to survive was to keep our guard up and maintain constant vigilance.

The instructor paused and looked over our group thoughtfully, waiting until we thought he was finished. We slowly began to walk away… and then he said, "By the way, one more thing. Since ground convoys are routinely slow, exposed, and cumbersome, they're among the enemy's favorite targets."

After that, he wished us good luck and walked away. It was unusual for one of the instructors to show up and give us a sendoff briefing. I've always remembered them for being so faithful to the challenge of transforming chicken hawks into eagles—and I hoped I'd become a little more than a crow.

The convoy officer took over, instructing us on what to do if any of the trucks hit a landmine or we were ambushed. He emphasized the importance of staying focused and never stopping our vehicles in a kill zone unless there was absolutely no alternative. The "Gun Truck," a tactical five-ton truck equipped with .50-caliber machine guns and fortified with steel plates, would help to keep the enemy at bay. For additional protection, two Huey gunships provided air cover throughout the trip. We mounted our vehicles, loaded our weapons, and headed for the gate.

A Walk in the Woods

We inched north at what seemed like a snail's pace, passing several Fire Support Bases along Thunder Road. One of the most well-known bases was Lai Khe, the headquarters of the 3rd Brigade, 1st Infantry Division. This sprawling complex included a massive airfield. Its proximity to supply deposits made it a logistical hub to support surrounding FSBs in Quan Loi, Phuoc Vinh, Dau Tieng, and the Special Forces camp at Loc Ninh.

Unfortunately, both Lai Khe and Loc Ninh were located near the infamous Iron Triangle, a well-known, heavily fortified area (with tunnels everywhere) used by Viet Cong and North Vietnamese forces as a logistical base and training area. Because Lai Khe posed a severe threat to communist interests, it drew regular mortar and rocket attacks. Lai Khe regularly got hit three to five times a day. As we passed Lai Khe, I noticed a sign at the main gate that read, "Welcome to Rocket City!"

It took most of the day to reach Quan Loi. Along the way, we observed the remnants of French colonial plantation life. Rice and rubber were Vietnam's main commodity exports, generating enormous profits for wealthy plantation owners, investors, and local officials.

One of the scouts, a South Vietnamese soldier, told me how the French-owned Michelin Tire Company continued to operate and make a fortune despite the war going on around them. When I asked how that was possible, he stroked his palms to illustrate the answer: *bribery*. Although France was an American ally, corporate groups like Michelin and individual French plantation owners financed the Viet Cong at a profit. Then, they turned around and bribed South Vietnamese officials to look the other way.

What a way to fight a war! Our leadership in Washington knew about this, too; it's how people did business in Southeast Asia. Like their counterparts in Saigon, American leaders simply turned a blind eye to all of this. You didn't find much in the way of servant leadership in those days, no matter where you looked.

Up Close and Personal

The only place I could observe true heroism, self-sacrifice, and servant leadership, it seemed, was the battlefield. It waited for me as soon as our convoy entered the gates of Quan Loi. Two CH-47 Chinook helicopters swooped in suddenly, hitting us with their powerful rotor blasts, sending Boonie hats and other loose items flying in all directions. It felt like being caught in a hurricane.

At first, I thought the pilots were playing games with us since we were new, and our jungle fatigues were a dead giveaway. But then, three Army ambulances rushed to the scene, and I realized the helicopters were carrying dead and wounded soldiers. I got a sobering reminder of the harsh realities that lay ahead. Everything my fellow veterans and instructors tried to prepare me for now appeared before my eyes. You don't truly understand it until you experience it for yourself.

The soldiers who returned alive and in one piece from battle looked like the walking dead. Their exhausted faces and worn-out uniforms, covered with red dust from the rough terrain, said it all. As they stepped off the Chinooks, I couldn't help but wonder about the physical and psychological toll war takes, even on the bravest of men. Several medics and ground crew jumped out of the ambulances and scurried back and forth to the Chinooks, carrying articles of equipment returned from battle.

When the last able-bodied trooper disembarked, four Army medics rushed in with urgency to tend to the wounded. They carried out three body bags, which they stacked near the rear hatch of a waiting ¾-ton truck. It was heart-wrenching. I couldn't help but feel a deep sense of sadness and despair. Would I share their fate? I had my first real war experience, and it stayed with me forever.

But I saw another side to this as I watched those medics and crew faithfully carry the remains of fallen comrades, doing their duty even though they possessed little hope of victory or peace. You could bet your bottom dollar those soldiers would be right back on the job the following day, no matter what Congress, the media, or anyone else said or did. Serving as a soldier teaches you to *keep going* long after you feel like you've reached a breaking point. I'd bet many of those men passed numerous breaking points. How many times could you do a job like that before your heart broke?

Somehow, at that moment, I understood that I was observing The Hope of War. It wasn't embodied in a president, a commanding general, or an act of Congress. It could only be seen through eyes of faith, in the simple courage of a handful of soldiers who did their jobs and risked their lives, whether they received a reward in this life or not. It's a pity so little leadership of this kind existed in Washington or Saigon... but it hadn't disappeared completely. If you knew where to look, you could find it.

Headquartered in Long Binh, the 90th Replacement Battalion deployed and repatriated all soldiers in and out of Vietnam during the war. Photo adapted from public domain.

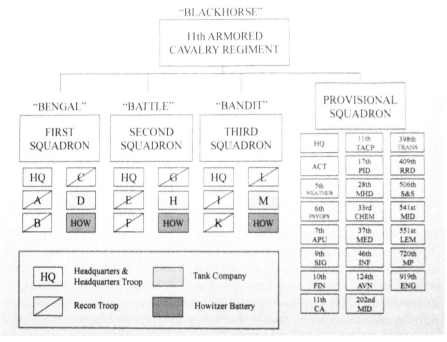

The 11th Armored Cavalry Regiment comprised three squadrons, a headquarters and headquarters troop (HHT), and an air cavalry troop. Each squadron had an HHT, three reconnaissance (Recon) troops, a tank company, and a howitzer battery. On average, each squadron had around 50 officers, six warrant officers, and 1,100 enlisted men, bringing the total number of personnel in the 11th Cav to approximately 3,600. The Regiment also had the support of other units, temporarily attached or placed under its operational control. With all these units combined, Blackhorse had a strength of over 4,500 men. The 11th Cav was a unique combined-arms force that could move, shoot, and communicate under a single commander.

Quan Loi Airfield and Forward Support Area (XT815904)

Quan Loi fire support base (FSB). The Viet Cong (VC) launched a massive rocket and mortar attack, followed by a sapper infiltration of the outer perimeter, just a few weeks before I arrived. Although temporarily overrun, troopers from the 1st Cavalry Division and the 11th Armored Cavalry eventually repelled the Viet Cong.

E Troop, from the 2nd Squadron of the 11th Armored Cavalry Regiment, pursued the enemy. As they did, they encountered a battalion-sized North Vietnamese (NVA) force. Ambushed from three sides, they suffered significant losses. The NVA killed or critically injured every single E Troop officer. The troop's ranking sergeant (E-5) took command, and later received the Distinguished Service Cross for his actions that day.

During the battle, H Company and the rest of the troops from the 2nd Squadron arrived to support E Troop's withdrawal. Rocket Propelled Grenades (RPGs) struck one of H Company's armored vehicles, severely injuring the officer on board and leaving him presumed dead. He managed to restart his vehicle and escape, and was later found and rescued. The Viet Cong captured another soldier, who was eventually released a few years later.

The battle lasted a full day, and more than 200 North Vietnamese Army soldiers died. I don't recall the number of U.S. casualties, but they were significant.

(Pictured Opposite)
When the 11th Armored Cavalry Regiment came ashore at the naval port at Vung Tau in September 1966, it faced a multitude of challenges besides the Viet Cong (VC) and the North Vietnamese Army (NVA). It also faced difficulties from Vietnam's rugged terrain and tropical climate, which adversely impacted the use of armored vehicles. The regiment's first year in Vietnam sharpened their combat skills. It gave them valuable experience fighting the enemy and time to acquaint themselves with the terrain. They learned how the weather could impact operations, and established foundations and tactics for counterinsurgency warfare. Map adapted from public domain.

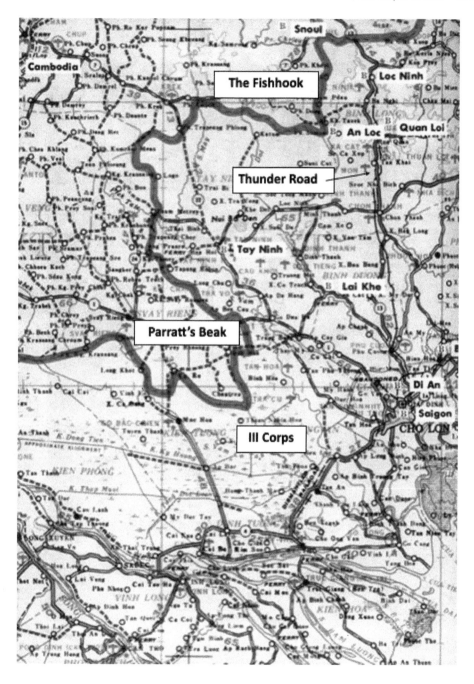

I arrived in Vietnam and plunged straight into the thick of things—the invasion of Cambodia. Despite limited time in-country, I witnessed firsthand the intensity and brutality of the conflict. The photograph to the left was taken one month after I arrived. Already, my uniform bore the marks of service. The oppressive heat and humidity of the jungle took their toll, causing my fatigues to wear out faster than anticipated. The photo opposite, taken one month later, shows the contrast, brought about by the harsh conditions under which we operated and the toll war takes on those who fight it.

The photograph captures a moment from mid-June 1970 at Fire Support Base (FSB) Bolan. It was located in no man's land south of An Loc in War Zone Charlie, which was a part of III Corps. During the monsoon season, life in Vietnam was excruciatingly difficult, but despite the challenging circumstances, the soldiers tried to find comfort in small pleasures such as a warm meal. Amidst the chaos and turmoil of war, the picture serves as a reminder to cherish the simple joys of life.

The U.S. and South Vietnamese governments believed Cambodia provided havens for the North Vietnamese Army and Viet Cong. The Cambodian head of state, Prince Norodom Sihanouk, and North Vietnamese leadership in Hanoi denied these allegations. In 1967, Western journalists uncovered an enemy base camp four miles inside "neutral" Cambodia. Three years later, the Pentagon green-lit restricted cross-border missions in Cambodia. These operations, to be carried out by U.S. and South Vietnamese forces, focused on two regions of the Cambodian border - the "Angel's Wing," or "Parrot's Beak," and the "Fishhook" regions. They aimed to seize or demolish enemy facilities and war materials. When President Richard Nixon ordered U.S. ground troops to invade Cambodia on April 28, 1970, he waited two days to announce that the Cambodian incursion had begun. With resentment already building domestically over the conflict in Vietnam, the incursion felt like a final straw. The news unleashed a wave of criticism and claims that the president had abused his powers by sidestepping Congress. By the time I reached Quan Loi in late May, the invasion of Cambodia was well underway. Photo adapted from the public domain.

The UH-1 "Huey" helicopter that carried Command Sergeant Major Robert Bolan, when enemy ground fire struck it and killed him on July 24, 1970. A mere two weeks remained before he was due to return home. The Squadron Commander at the time, Colonel Don Starry, miraculously survived the crash. He later rose to the rank of four-star general and served as the commanding general of the United States Army Armor Center and School, as well as the commander of V Corps in the Federal Republic of Germany from 1976 to 1977.

Chapter Ten
The War That Shaped Me

**Rarely can you apprehend the changes you go through until
long after the process is complete. What felt like pressure, pain,
and sorrow for me in Vietnam feels very different now.
One day, you'll reflect on seemingly hopeless and futile situations
and exclaim with other veterans,
"It was the 'best and worst of times' of my life!"**

Cambodia's neutrality and vulnerability made it a "safe zone" for North Vietnamese attacks. General Creighton Abrams eagerly waited for a chance to put a stop to this treachery, and the opportunity came in March 1970 with the overthrow of Prince Norodom Sihanouk, who tolerated North Vietnam's secret bases. The coup installed a more U.S.-friendly government under Marshal Lon Nol, a politician and military general. Lon reversed course and allowed American and South Vietnamese forces to strike the communist havens.[1]

The anti-war movement roared to life in outrage and indignation. Protests intensified nationwide, particularly on college campuses. One hundred thousand people marched on Washington. Nearly four hundred schools went on strike, and over two hundred closed completely. On May 4th, protests turned violent: National Guardsmen fired on anti-war demonstrators at Ohio's Kent State University, killing four students and wounding nine. Ten days later, two students were killed at Jackson State University. The unrest galvanized the left against the Cambodian incursion.[2]

Meanwhile, in Washington, the U.S. Senate approved the Cooper-Church Amendment by a vote of seventy-eight to eleven. It prohibited U.S. combat troops or advisers from operating in Laos or Thailand, and, for the first time, Congress found the votes to limit the president's ability to wage war in Vietnam. The Senate also repealed the Gulf of Tonkin Resolution by a vote of eighty-one to ten, reasserting control over the executive branch. That December, Congress passed an enhanced version of the Cooper-Church Amendment. Neither action stopped the bombing campaigns in Laos or Cambodia.[3]

President Richard Nixon felt besieged on all sides. He believed Democrats in Congress covertly plotted the demise of his presidency. The Senate rejected two of his Supreme Court nominations, which Nixon took as public humiliation. In February, news leaked to the media about the "secret war" in Laos. When they questioned Henry Kissinger about whether the story was true, he denied that any Americans had been killed while fighting in Laos. Two days later, the press learned that twenty-seven Americans had died there. Nixon's approval rating plummeted by eleven points.[4]

Nixon's decision to expand the Vietnam War into Cambodia and Laos had predictable consequences. Many in Congress, as well as anti-war activists and college students across the country, claimed that he lied to the American people to win the presidency. He promised to end the war, but now he was escalating it by invading two neutral countries. They framed it as antithetical to his pledge and inferred that the war might continue for several more years. Aware that he sat at another crossroads, Nixon again turned to the Silent Majority. During a nationally televised address, he presented the nation with the choice at hand, exposed his antagonists for who they were, and left it to the people to decide.

Once again, Nixon survived the crossroads; the public continued to support him. The address bought him some time, which he used to aggressively seek an end to the war. From 1970-73, the U.S. progressively "took the gloves off" with North Vietnam and pummeled them into submission. The American people approved, propelling Nixon to a landslide victory over his Democratic challenger, George McGovern, in the 1972 presidential election. Nixon won 60.7% of the popular and 520 electoral votes, while McGovern won only 37.5% and seventeen electoral votes. Nixon's victory margin of nearly eighteen million votes remains the largest in history to this day.[5]

When to Hold 'Em and When to Fold 'Em

The communists also sensed that time was running out. Buoyed by the controversies over incursions into Cambodia and Laos, they attempted the Easter Offensive, an all-out invasion of South Vietnam on March 30, 1972. At first, it seemed to work; South Vietnamese forces suffered staggering defeats. Then, the U.S. unleashed Operation *Linebacker*—a massive aerial bombardment of North Vietnam. They mined Haiphong Harbor, Hanoi's principal entry point for Soviet seaborne supplies, and ordered hundreds of U.S. aircraft into action against Northern forces and their supply lines. By mid-June, the communists' Easter Offensive had ground to a halt. They were overwhelmed, cut off from resupply, and completely outmatched.

Perhaps North Vietnamese leaders remembered the wisdom of communist godfather Vladimir Lenin: "Probe with bayonets; if you find mush, push; if you find steel, withdraw." Between the shellacking they took at home and the beatings we gave them in Cambodia and Laos, it was more than the North could bear. Aware of Nixon's recent rapport-building measures with the Soviet Union and China, they came to the negotiating table at the urging of Soviet leader Leonid Brezhnev. In October 1972, Kissinger and North Vietnamese leader Le Duc Tho began work on a fragile peace accord based on two concessions: the U.S. would not insist on a complete withdrawal of North Vietnamese troops from South Vietnam, and North Vietnam would not insist on new leadership to replace South Vietnamese leader Nguyen Van Thieu.

On January 27, 1973, representatives of the South Vietnamese communist forces, North Vietnam, South Vietnam, and the United States, signed the Agreement on Ending the War and Restoring Peace in Vietnam. Within sixty days of the agreement, all U.S. forces would be withdrawn, all U.S. bases dismantled, and all prisoners of war (POWs) released. America's part in the Vietnam War was over; Nixon had achieved a military and political victory.

Or so it seemed. The U.S. Senate, controlled by the opposition party and still under the spell of the media and the anti-war movement, refused to ratify the treaty. Fighting between North and South Vietnam continued almost immediately after they signed the treaty and for a further year until the fall of Saigon and the conquest of South Vietnam in April 1975. The media threw an ocean's worth of gasoline on the fire of the Watergate Scandal for the remainder of Nixon's presidency, which made it all but impossible for the fragile peace to truly take root.

Snatching Defeat from the Jaws of Victory

In his book, *The Nixon Conspiracy*, Geoff Shepard points out how deeply the mainstream media and Washington ruling class despised Nixon. The successes in Cambodia, Laos, and Operation *Linebacker* led to the largest, most lopsided presidential contest in U.S. history. It spoke volumes about what the nation could achieve when it stood on principle rather than politics. It exposed how *un*-popular the anti-war movement was, how little impact it honestly had, and how few Americans truly wanted to "cut and run" from defeating communism. In some cases, it threatened several legislators' credibility and re-election chances. In my opinion, the Senate's refusal to ratify Nixon's treaty showed how little they truly cared about peace.

Politics doesn't simply go away because you stand on principle. The nonstop drumbeat of the press, anti-war activists, and Congress shifted their focus to Nixon's fatal weakness—his paranoia. Since they failed to defeat him at the ballot box, they turned to a different tactic: delegitimizing his presidency. They exposed corruption among members of his re-election campaign in the form of a break-in to the Democratic Party Headquarters at the Watergate Office Building in Washington. Nixon spent the majority of his second term fighting off allegations of cover-up by his administration, and he resigned on August 8, 1974, before he could be impeached by Congress.

We all encounter pivotal moments where the decisions we make shape our legacy. President Nixon made a lot of good decisions... but also some bad ones. Ironically, the bad decisions that precipitated his downfall were utterly unnecessary; he'd received a massive vote of confidence from the American people. In hindsight, the Nixon campaign had no call to resort to the tactics they used. Fear of losing and hampering their progress got the better of them. Nixon's failure to come clean about it early on cost him his second term and (to some extent) his legacy.

Sometimes, the most difficult thing to see clearly is when we're doing *well*. Mostly, it takes place away from the bright lights, with little to no applause. We improve in the shadows, growing, staying the course, mastering complex tasks, and refusing to give in to enormous pressure. We operate at our best when the chips are down and with our backs against the wall. If we persevere, we can reap considerable rewards, as Nixon did on election day. But if we surrender to our fear (as Nixon did), we compromise our integrity and multiply our problems. When difficulties chafe against our souls, instead of crying out for relief and certainty, we should learn to embrace the storm—to dance in it, as they say.

Storms pass more quickly for people who keep dancing and keep moving. The longer you sit still and let them wreak their havoc, the longer they last, and the more prone you become to making bad decisions. But if you get up and move and make use of your agency as a human being, you get through them faster. For me, several pivotal moments occurred during my tour in Vietnam because no matter what came along, I *kept moving forward*—for God's glory. My faith grew stronger, my convictions deeper, and I developed profound empathy for others, allowing me to see the world through God's eyes. I didn't fully understand this as it happened, either. If you'd asked me then, I would have said I was "just doing my job." But the longer I kept at it, the more comfortable I became with dancing in the storm.

The Sharp End of the Stick

I received an assignment to the 11th Cavalry Regiment, a unit rich with history from fighting in seven significant conflicts and wars. When I arrived, its 2nd Squadron had been engaging the enemy across the Cambodian border for three weeks.

General Abrams' strategy of disrupting communist operations in Cambodia and Laos worked. The Viet Cong and North Vietnamese Army (NVA) used a network of trails, a vital lifeline flowing from sanctuary bases inside Cambodia, to sustain combat operations in South Vietnam. The Cambodia invasion was a combined U.S. and South Vietnamese operation focused on the southern border at what was called the "Parrot's Beak" and the "Fishhook," both well-known enemy strongholds.

With recent Cambodian political developments tilting in General Abrams's favor, he launched the attack by airlifting U.S. airmobile infantry and AVRN paratroopers twenty kilometers inside the Fishhook as a blocking force. Then, the 2nd Squadron and their ARVN counterparts charged across the Cambodian border, pushing units of the 7th NVA Division into the waiting guns of the infantry and helicopter gunships. The movement took the enemy entirely by surprise, causing them to scatter, leaving behind their half-eaten breakfast, laundry, and stockpiles of military supplies and equipment. Afterward, the 1st and 2nd Squadrons moved back across the border just south of the Fishhook, while the 3rd Squadron moved near Lai Khe.

The NVA failed to establish an air defense network around sanctuary bases. Air cavalry helicopter gunships roamed the skies ahead of our advance, looking for the enemy and shooting anything that moved. The tactical surprise came thanks to our network of agents —brave souls who risked their lives to feed sensitive information to squadron intelligence—dispersed throughout the region. Captured enemy documents revealed how the assault put NVA forces in total disarray, forcing them to retreat into the interior of Cambodia to survive. In the end, we killed, wounded, or captured almost nine thousand enemy soldiers, fourteen million pounds of rice, and vast stores of munitions, weapons, and medical supplies. (In his June 3rd television address to the nation, President Nixon used footage of stockpiles that looked a lot like the ones we gathered.)

In fifty-nine days of combat, the 11th Cavalry did what no other unit could have done in such a short period. The tragic loss to the regiment was 40 Blackhorse troopers killed and 322 wounded. Their action in Cambodia from May 1 to June 29 earned troopers the prestigious Presidential Unit Citation for Valor.

Growing Up Quickly

Cambodia was my first and most significant combat operation in Vietnam, where I came face-to-face with bombs and bullets and survived. All my subsequent encounters consisted of chance confrontations with the enemy, brief skirmishes, mortar, and rocket attacks, treacherous weather, and navigating the unforgiving terrain. As a nervous teenager, the Cambodian operation was my "baptism of fire." It gave me a taste of an operation's demands, uncertainties, and flow—while I advanced across unfamiliar territory with a fierce enemy lurking in the shadows of dense jungle.

The main challenge of the operation was asset delivery. My platoon worked around the clock, dealing with "combat emergencies" almost daily. We were responsible for delivering supplies to scouts and infantry, ensuring they reached the right unit at the right time and the correct grid location on the map. The operation was fast-paced, and precision was crucial. I had plenty of doubts, fears, and weaknesses as I went into battle.

The regiment consisted of three combat squadrons containing three tank companies, three howitzer batteries, a helicopter air cavalry troop, and twenty-three provisional units such as engineers, medical, communications, and chemical. If we had an Achilles' heel, it was in the wheelhouse of logistics—resupply, recovery, and maintenance. Fulfilling them required considerable forethought by regiment staff before they committed to an operation. They had to survey existing logistical support within a specific area and compare it against anticipated needs. If they couldn't support themselves during a mission... they wouldn't be much use in supporting the combat units. They'd have to find other ways to keep the fighters fed, watered, and supplied. These "other ways" often involved truck convoys to shuttle supplies and munitions from Long Binh to forward locations.

When you think of war heroes, do you picture truck drivers? That was us: the lifeline between the combat units and the supplies. Truck convoys were prime enemy targets. Troopers assigned to the HHT transportation platoon trained to be front-line soldiers. Like transport soldiers in Iraq and Afghanistan, truckers in Vietnam got hit by improvised explosive devices (IEDs) and small arms attacks by guerrilla forces. We had to stay ready to assault and retaliate while on the move.

The Pain We Felt Together

One day, I noticed one of the lead "Kit Carson" scouts among a group of Blackhorse troops waiting to catch a helicopter flight to a forward firebase. Kit Carson scouts were usually former communist soldiers who defected to South Vietnam and volunteered to fight alongside Allied forces. Generally, Blackhorse troopers tended to look down on regular ARVN troops as an inferior fighting force. But the elite units, such as ARVN airborne, ranger, and marine battalions, commanded our respect. The Kit Carson fighters were even more so; you could imagine what would happen to them as defectors if the communists captured them in battle.

I walked over to the scout and struck up a conversation. Initially, he showed surprise but opened up when he recognized my genuine interest in his thoughts and opinions. What he shared exposed the dilemma of the South Vietnamese people, and I felt a tremendous sense of empathy for their plight.

He told me the Viet Cong had come to his village one night, looking for recruits. When his father refused to allow him and his younger brother to join them, they threatened to kill his entire family of twelve. A year later, his younger brother was killed during the Tet Offensive. He eventually learned that the Viet Cong had murdered his whole family because his father refused to give them his share of the annual rice harvest. So, he defected to the South, eventually linking up with the 11th Cavalry.

That day, I learned the power of conversations for personal growth and connecting with people, provided you're willing to listen to the other person's point of view. Wars often happen because people stop communicating with each other. We'll find merit and reward in laying aside prejudices and stereotypes to see others as God sees them.

I never saw that scout again and often wondered whether he survived the war. But I never forgot what he shared with me.

Elsewhere, I sustained a minor injury that required surgery at Long Binh Army Hospital, which was understaffed due to recent troop withdrawals. I recovered in a ward with several injured patients. To the left and right of me were two gunners from a Navy gunboat crew who'd been ambushed while on patrol in the Mekong Delta. Across from me lay the boat's chief. The crew's coxswain was in the ICU with a critical head wound, and the doctors were doing everything they could to stabilize him so he could be evacuated to a hospital in Japan. My three new friends were riddled with shrapnel wounds that drained constantly, requiring attention every few hours. The hospital didn't have enough nurses to care for all the patients, so I volunteered to change bandages and bed linens.

One medical ward over from me, a South Vietnamese soldier lay groaning in pain. The blast of a landmine had hit him, and shrapnel had claimed both legs. He suffered terribly and howled with misery. One of the medics started mocking the ARVN soldier and telling him to "Shut the hell up!" Immediately, I intervened. I shouted at the medic, "Knock it off and take care of your patient!" The hospital staff was being pushed to the limits of their endurance, but that was no excuse for kicking a man when he was down. I know how easily you can lose touch with reality; your sense of empathy vanishes quickly. That's another of the enemy's tricks—to get you to feel sorry for yourself. The best way to fight back is to roll up your sleeves and serve the less fortunate, and trust me, it will change your attitude quickly!

Smiling Back at Death

The Cambodian incursion, codenamed Operation *Menu*, came to a successful conclusion in June 1970. After Cambodia, armored reconnaissance platoons of the 2nd Squadron moved into the vicinity of An Loc, west of Quan Loi and War Zone Charlie. It's where I had one of my top three closest encounters with death.

The town of An Loc emerged from nineteenth-century French Colonialism, carved out of a jungle wilderness by indigenous people known to the French as the Montagnard ("mountain dweller"). Eventually, it became the operations center for the vast Michelin Tire empire. Their headquarters was built on the surrounding heights, much like the walled fortress towns of medieval Europe. The walls surrounding An Loc were far less imposing, constructed mainly of bricks and stucco, with four gates that provided the only barriers to defend against enemy forces. Around An Loc was a network of well-worn trails moderating from Cambodia into South Vietnam. Several of our recon platoons operated in the general areas and further south in War Zone Charlie. Our job was to move cargo to support the squadrons from Quan Loi to forward FBSs.

We maneuvered through a routine mission with no apparent enemy threats. But when our turn came to unload, my companion stepped on a tripwire attached to a booby trap.

Thankfully, it was a dud. One of the Kit Carson scouts destroyed the device, which turned out to be a U.S. fragmentary grenade rigged with a tripwire. After quickly checking the surrounding area, they gave us the "all clear" to resume unloading. I didn't think about it then, but later that night, I remembered how quickly things can change in war. The moment you let your guard down, the enemy is most likely to strike. On any other day, it could have been a lot worse.

Almost Dead, Again

In December 1970, the 2nd Squadron returned to Camp Di An for an official standdown. It was a time to refit, regroup, and replenish our battered vehicles and worn-out equipment. We took advantage of the standdown for repairs, overhauls, and cleaning. Someone hatched the hare-brained idea of creating a makeshift ammo dump near the troopers' temporary living area, and then he ordered my platoon to collect all the loose munitions and take them there.

It didn't take a rocket scientist to realize how unsafe this was! We placed mounds of unsecured ammo on pallets encircled by only a four-foot wall of sandbags. As I left the ammo dump, I heard a loud popping noise. Looking to my side, I saw smoke from a white phosphorous grenade and realized it was causing munitions to explode from the intense heat. I yelled for everyone to run away from the ammo dump as fast as possible. A massive explosion went off, knocking us to the ground. After a quick head count, we realized one of our companions was missing. We thought he'd been killed. We moved to a safer location, and then we saw our missing friend running across a field, terrified out of his mind. He was due to rotate home soon, and we could see how very relieved he felt to have survived. All he could say was, "Thank you, Jesus!"

Here, I experienced my second close brush with death—albeit this time, it was somewhat self-inflicted.

The Last Mission

After eight months in Vietnam, I'd become an adrenaline junkie, hooked on the challenge of roaming the badlands in pursuit of an elusive enemy. It was "all fun and games until someone got hurt." A rumor circulated that Echo and Fox Troops would depart from the Ho Bo Woods for a mission southeast of Saigon. I eagerly wanted to join; I'd heard that the breathtaking coastal regions of South Vietnam could compete with some of the world's most well-known resorts (and that turned out to be true).

I informed my platoon leader, First Lieutenant Bruno, that I wanted to participate in the upcoming mission, as it would probably be my last before going home. I preferred being in the mix of things over spending the next four months at Camp Di An fighting off the daily boredom. After several days, he told me to pack my gear and catch the first helicopter to Firebase Ham Tan.

FBS Ham Tan was nothing more than a series of outer and inner dirt berms used for protection against enemy mortar and rocket attacks. The firebase covered an area of about three acres and was void of any wooden structures, indicating the primitive living conditions of its former occupants. Echo Troop held the temporary responsibility for securing the base. However, after Echo Troop left, we had to rely on an artillery battery, two armored cavalry assault vehicles (ACAVs), and one Sheridan battle tank to keep the main access road between Ham Tan and Highway 1 open, for this road was the only way to receive supplies from Long Binh other than by air.

Target: Cripps

At this point in the war, we never left anything on the battlefield that the enemy could use to injure or kill us. We *always* picked up everything and took it back to base. (The Viet Cong were masters at reconfiguring ordinary items into booby traps). During one push through a dense jungle area, an ACAV from Fox Troop hit a landmine. I volunteered to lead the team in recovering it, with assistance from a CH-54-B Skycrane, the Army's largest and most powerful heavy-lifting helicopter.

The end of my tour was near. I had no business participating in that recovery mission, but I did it anyway. We arrived late in the afternoon and hiked for about half an hour to reach the damaged ACAV. I rigged it for extraction while the squad spread out in a defensive position. I focused so much on my work that when it happened, I neither heard nor saw it: an enemy sniper round hit the dirt *directly behind me.* Suddenly, someone shouted, "A sniper in the tree line!" I'd dodged being picked off by about two feet!

We called for a "hunter-killer" backup. Hunter-killer helicopters operated in pairs—one aimed to spot and identify the enemy (the hunter), and the other launched the attack (the killer). We had a hunter-killer team hovering out of sight, ready to pounce on command. I told the radio operator to call for backup. We heard the Hueys as they passed by, and that was the last we heard from our uninvited friend.

The Long Way Home

A few weeks later, three more of my friends died when their ACAV hit a landmine. I had held in my grief since Lynn West's death, but the deaths of three friends at this late stage in the war opened the floodgates of bitterness, anger, and frustration. Those guys were almost home! That night, I found a secluded place and cried my eyes out. (Keep this skill fresh and handy when you're in combat. Even the toughest souls need to grieve.)

I wasn't even twenty years old, and now I held the title of a Vietnam Veteran, a warrior who'd risked his neck, dodged bullets, fought a savage enemy, and survived. I had become a man others could depend on. I'd joined the hallowed ranks of a combat warrior where men I deeply admired, like my father and Lynn, already had their places. But I had lingering questions that I wouldn't be able to answer for many years. Why had I been lucky enough to survive? Why couldn't my buddies be with me? How did I get a pass to go home when they didn't? Why couldn't we have all come home together?

In the weeks before it was time for me to rotate home, the squadron held an awards ceremony to recognize the contributions some of us had made during our tour as a Blackhorse Trooper. Emotions ran high in the aftermath of the event as we promised one another to meet again, knowing all along we probably never would. The brotherhood forged among combatants in war is a memory civilians will never fully understand or appreciate. The sentimentality overflows because you remember what you endured... and who you endured it with.

Another mystery I was yet to embrace was how much of a change I had undergone since entering the Army. If I changed drastically in one summer working for Roger Underwood, how much more after two years of military service, including my tour in Vietnam? I had a simple plan—to return home, enter college, find work, and get on with my life. But another trap lay in wait: the world I was now leaving in Vietnam and the world of my adolescence I'd already left behind headed toward each other on a collision course. I faced a new challenge, unaware of the demands of readjusting to the safety, simplicity, and reduced intensity of returning home. In hindsight, I felt more prepared for that sniper near Ham Tan than for the emotional struggle of reintegration that no one told me about or prepared me for.

If anything felt more futile than fighting a war we wouldn't win, it was returning to civilian life in the U.S. and pretending everything I'd been through was "in the past." But I tried to do it … in some ways, for another thirty years. I believe many fellow veterans of wars, past and present, face similar problems. How do you go from a lifestyle of intense, thrilling, and purposeful camaraderie on the road back to average American life? How do you go from pain, sorrow, heartbreak, and loss to climbing the corporate ladder and keeping up with the Joneses? Maybe it doesn't sound like a challenge... but if you try living through it, you'll see what I mean.

Upon reflection, I realized that the skills and experience I acquired during my training and service in Vietnam played a crucial role in helping me overcome the difficulties of reintegrating into society. While in combat, I learned an invaluable lesson that has stayed with me throughout my life - never give up, no matter how complex or dire the situation may appear. I had to persevere and remain steadfast in my commitment to serve those who relied on me for support. After over three decades of keeping my experiences in Vietnam bottled up, I finally acknowledged the impact the war had on me. This admission granted me peace and allowed me to begin the healing process for my soul. I now have a better understanding of how to guide others who have gone through combat trauma and can serve as an example to the upcoming generation of warriors.

One thing I am sure of is that if you are honest with yourself and the Lord about any past hurts, no matter what they may be, the emotional distress will eventually pass. It is similar to every other storm that you might have faced in your life. And once the clouds clear and the sun shines, you will find even more of *The Hope of War*.

These are pictures of the remains of the 2nd Squadron ammo dump at Camp Di An. In early 1971, during our operations standdown, a white phosphorus grenade accidentally went off. This caused a chain reaction that triggered a massive explosion, destroying several buildings, including the roof of the Regiment Chapel (see below),

which can be seen in the background of the second photo. Fortunately, no one was killed, but several people were injured from the blast and flying debris. Six Blackhorse troopers, including myself, escaped the dump just before the explosion. Personal photos.

By the late fall of 1970, Blackhorse Troopers of the 2nd Squadron continued to successfully keep the enemy from reopening his infiltration routes and resupply along Serge's Jungle Highway and the Saigon-Michelin Corridor, giving U.S. MACV-Advisory Teams to strengthen pacification efforts throughout the countryside. Over the next 90 days, Blackhorse Troopers made the lives of the few Viet Cong and NVA forces remaining between Tay Ninh and the Cambodian border a living hell. The photo shows a Fox Troop on patrol within War Zone "C." Personal photo.

The Vietnam War had a devastating impact on people from all walks of life, including children. The war years were particularly difficult for children in both North and South Vietnam. Many children lost their homes, and those who managed to receive an education had to attend classes after dark to avoid being targeted by the Viet Cong. The Communists often forced children as

young as 13 or 14 to participate in guerrilla warfare against American and South Vietnamese soldiers. They also used them as informants, making distinguishing between friends and foes difficult. While at FSB Ham Tan, children from the adjacent Ham Tan District frequently visited the firebase water collecting point on the nearby river or around the airfield, seeking help. Therefore, I always made it a point to keep a case of C-rations or candy to give them whenever they came. There was a little boy among those children who grew quite fond of me, and he can be seen in the picture. Personal photo.

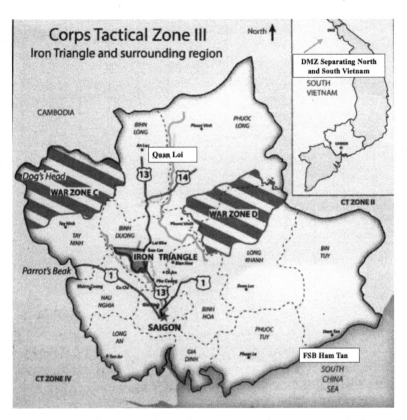

After the Cambodia campaign, the 2nd Squadron operated through III Corps under the operational control (OPCON) of the Third Brigade Task Force of the 1st Cavalry Division (Airmobile). As modern-day cavalrymen, Blackhorse troopers lived in their Armored Cavalry Assault Vehicles (ACAVs), M-48 Patton Tanks, M551 Sheridan light tanks, mechanized Howitzer vehicles, Command Post Vehicles, and UH-1 Huey and OH-6A scout helicopters seven days a week. The Regiment was 100 percent mobile with its organic equipment, meaning it was fundamentally self-sufficient and didn't have to rely on other combat arms units for support.   However, the Regiment's Achilles heel was in logistics, which required moving massive amounts daily to operate and change the NVA and Viet Cong around the boundaries of III Corps. My platoon's job was to keep the flow of supplies moving by whatever means available. Map adapted from public domain.

AH-1 Cobra Attack Helicopter

During the Vietnam War, hunter-killer tactics were used to revolutionize aerial reconnaissance and ground attack operations. Smaller, agile helicopters like the OH-6 Cayuse, nicknamed "Loach," identified and marked targets, while heavily armed helicopters like the AH-1 Cobra neutralized threats with weapons. The hunter-killer tactic was innovative and effective in the challenging combat conditions of Vietnam, particularly given the dense jungle terrain and the often elusive Viet Cong guerrillas. However, the close-proximity flying style of the scout helicopters made them vulnerable to enemy fire, and many were shot down or damaged during the conflict. As the war progressed and anti-aircraft weaponry became more prevalent among North Vietnamese forces, the hunter-killer tactic faced challenges, requiring adaptations in strategy and technology. Air Cavalry Troop, 11th Armored Cavalry Regiment photo.

The OH-6 Cayuse is nicknamed "Loach"
(from LOH, Light Observation Helicopter)

This is a photo of me at FSB Ham Tan preparing to connect a combat sortie using a Boeing CH-47 Chinook helicopter, which was, at the time, the Army's primary heavy lifter aircraft for transporting troops and supplies. By 1971, the U.S. Army had 21 Chinook companies operating in Vietnam, and a total of about 200 Chinook were lost either in combat or due to operational accidents during the war. Below is me hooking the cargo. Personal photos.

This is a photo of my dear friend Army CPT Stan Corvin Jr. during his first of two tours in Vietnam between 1968-69 and 1971-72. Stan was a part of the 71st Assault Helicopter Company, also known as "The Rattlers," based in Chu Lai in I Corps. During his first mission, Stan had to retrieve the bodies of nine American soldiers who were killed in a fierce battle with the NVA. This experience was his first exposure to the harsh reality of war, and according to Stan, it didn't prepare him for the challenges he would face in the future. On this mission, Stan is riding the left seat in a Loach helicopter. He's holding an M-60 machine gun, which means he's flying a shotgun. The M-60 was used to suppress enemy ground fire and make them duck for cover.

This picture shows two UH-1 Huey helicopter gunship pilots following an awards ceremony in which the pilot on the left received the Silver Star Medal. These two young officers were part of A Company 82nd Aviation Battalion, known as the "Cowboys." In September 1966, A/82nd was re-designated the 335th Aviation Company (Airmobile Light) and eventually the 335th Assault Helicopter Company. My Uncle Lynn West served with the Cowboys during his first tour in Vietnam, 1965-66.

The young helicopter pilots during the Vietnam War era shared many similarities with their World War II fighter pilot counterparts. They were confident, bold, and daring, emanating a level of self-assurance that was unmatched. Despite their constant daily danger, they never complained and faced their fears head-on. These pilots recognized that the lives of soldiers on the ground depended on them, which made them dependable and reliable. Their unwavering commitment to their mission and bravery made them the most unstoppable force in the Vietnam War. Photos adapted from the public domain.

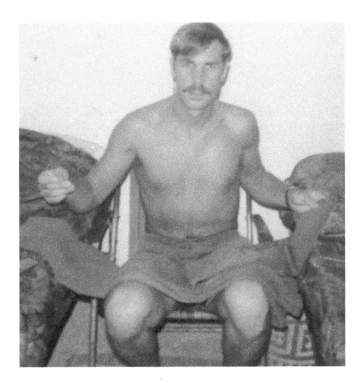

My military uniforms had become worn out and frayed at this point in my tour. Despite their condition, I took it upon myself to mend them as best I could. I spent hours sewing and patching up my jungle fatigues, hoping to make them presentable enough for my upcoming journey to Camp Di An. My orders were waiting for me there, signaling my transfer to the 90th Replacement Battalion and, eventually, a trip to Travis Air Force Base in California. I was counting down the weeks, but there was still a war on, so I tried to remain focused on the matter at hand.

Left to right: SP/4 Neal Bainter, PVT Frank Marcantonio, and SGT Bill Wilhelm died in combat near FSB Ham Tan when their ACAV hit a hand-controlled landmine. ARVN engineers cleared the road for mines early that morning, but this one slipped past them. Sergeant Wilhelm and crew headed to the firebase watering point on a nearby river to provide security, when the landmine struck. Neal and Frank died instantly, but Bill lingered for two days before succumbing to his wounds. With people constantly moving about, you never knew when Viet Cong insurgents hid among us. I managed losses reasonably well up to this point, but the death of three friends so late in the war brought me to tears. There was no holding back the grief, so later that evening, I slipped away from everyone else and sobbed my heart out. Photos adapted from the public domain.

During the ACAV recovery mission, a second Huey was deployed as an escort. Although there were other members of the platoon who could have led the squad, most of them were new and needed to gain experience. Therefore, being the most experienced, I decided to take charge. However, my decision was not without reservations, as my brother Fred had advised me against volunteering for anything towards the end of my tour. Despite this, I took on the responsibility and led the squad and found myself in the crosshairs of an enemy sniper. I should have listened to Fred and played it safe, but my reckless nature got the best of me.

Chapter Eleven
The Years of Transition

Dreams usually appear long before they become reality. In the period between the birth of a dream and its realization, you'll experience doubts, obstacles, unexpected changes, and surprises. Don't give up on your dreams just because life doesn't seem to make sense. It always makes sense to God, and your dreams matter to Him.

The sun moves westward at approximately one thousand miles per hour. My flight from Bien Hoa Airbase in South Vietnam moved eastward at five hundred miles per hour. We reached Travis Air Force Base in California the same day we left Vietnam, though the flight lasted sixteen hours or more. Sometimes, when you fly from Southeast Asia or Australia to the western U.S., you "land before you take off," chronologically. (It's weird how that works.) After the first leg of our journey, we began to experience disorientation from crossing the International Date Line. We were jet lagged, but at least we were headed home!

Looking around the cabin, I saw the exhaustion of war in the faces of the young men. Many spent long hours on foot patrols searching for an elusive enemy or hiding in dense jungle overgrowth waiting for him in ambush. Some had spent months on tanks and ACAVs, traveling Vietnam's diverse and unforgiving terrain and weather. Others fought boredom and monotony from being "in the rear, with the gear." Very slowly, the prospect of life beyond Vietnam began to overshadow the memories of all the hardships most of us had endured.

The atmosphere on the flight crackled with energy. It seemed like people wanted to talk about anything *except* Vietnam. The men spoke of their long-term plans, such as completing college, getting married, finding jobs, or starting businesses. They also talked about their short-term plans—the "first thing I'm going to do when I get home" kind of plans.

They also ate like they hadn't eaten for several weeks. The flight attendants provided us with ample food and treats, and when they ran low, the soldiers asked about leftovers that other passengers hadn't eaten. So much for C-rations! The men were so emotionally charged that it was difficult to sleep. We'd made it past our time in "hell," and the journey home sparked feelings of irrepressible joy!

What Had I Learned?

I took time to reflect on my experiences in Vietnam, sort of like taking an "inventory" of the reality I brought back with me. I certainly wasn't the "Nineteen-and-Green" rookie I'd been when I left, but… who had I become? I couldn't express it in a single sentence. Nowadays, as an older man, I can see why, in hindsight, I struggled to put words to it.

Like law enforcement, soldiers who fight wars operate at *abnormal* levels. They deal daily with situations they're not used to and which most civilians never have to face. If you have a quiet combat veteran in your family who never talks about their experiences, it will help you to think of their transition as a "wilderness" season where they have a priority of finding *clues* rather than closure.

Veterans who battle conditions like post-traumatic stress disorder and operational/combat stress reactions don't always understand everything they're going through all at once. They face a journey of discovery. It's a frustrating process; they often feel like they're getting nowhere, fast. That's okay. The journey needs to give them time to find the words to communicate what they lived through. If that's happening for someone you love, think of it this way: you'll speak a lot louder with your *ears* than with your mouth. Your prayers and presence are the best gifts you can give to a struggling combat veteran.

I would need a lot of time to process the residual effects of Vietnam on my soul. But I understood other things right away as I sat in my seat on that plane, reflecting on my tour in Vietnam.

I remembered the day I first arrived at Quan Loi and how nervous I felt about my ability to perform under pressure. Everything about the journey ahead felt like unknown territory at that point, and I wondered if I would fail. But the bravery I witnessed from the medics who rushed out to carry wounded soldiers from the Chinooks gave me enough courage to keep going. I somehow knew—I wouldn't find an abundance of hope everywhere I looked. Instead, I would have to look for it in the *tiniest traces* of goodness. I would have to get down on my hands and knees, so to speak, and look as closely as I could.

If something difficult came along, I knew what to consider if I wanted to find hope. Could I walk? Could I see? Did I have ten fingers and toes? Could I breathe properly? Did I have people who loved me? Some, like those men in the hospital whose bandages I changed, didn't even have those! I knew men who'd lost limbs and eyesight and who couldn't breathe without the help of machines. I knew men who would have preferred to remain in Vietnam because, at least there, they had brothers who cared about them; they had no families waiting for them back in the States. When you think hope is lost, start with the simplest forms of goodness in your life and build on them with everything you've got.

I thought about the Blackhorse troopers and how deeply we cared for each other, even if we didn't have the best personal chemistry. Some of us were more likable than others, but *everyone* understood that the only way to survive was to work together. We treated each other with respect, whether we felt like it or not. Christian love is the same way; it can't be based on feelings because feelings come and go. We must make conscious choices to override our feelings in the service of God's Kingdom. As Hall of Fame NFL coach Vince Lombardi said:

If you're going to play together as a team, you've got to care for one another. You've got to love each other. Each player has to think about the next guy and say to himself: If I don't block that man,

Paul is going to get his legs broken. I have to do my job well so that he can do his. The difference between mediocrity and greatness is the feeling these guys have for each other.

I also learned to avoid complaining about anything beyond my control. When things get tough, roll up your sleeves and go to work. We stayed so busy in Vietnam that we didn't have time to feel sorry for ourselves. Even if we did, it wouldn't have made any difference—so why waste time? When hardship and sorrow abound, fight to remember the difference between what you control versus what you don't.

Welcome Home, Vietnam Veteran

We landed at Travis Air Force Base around 8:00 a.m. on a Thursday, and commercial buses waited to take us to the Army Overseas Replacement Center in Oakland. Our homecoming was unceremonious. We had struggled to survive for a year in a cause that had long since lost its luster, and no one came out to greet us or offer any recognition. After a year of carrying out missions for Uncle Sam, most of us had only one objective—to get discharged from the Army, leave Vietnam behind, and move on.

Soldiers who continued their service in the Army had a brief layover in Oakland before they could return home on leave. The rest of us were set to go through a two-day process of paperwork, pre-discharge medical exams, and meetings with officials from the Department of Veterans Affairs. For our final step, we had to get fitted with the Army Class "A" dress uniform, which was mandatory attire for commercial travel at that time. When I arrived in Vietnam, I weighed 210 pounds. By the end of my tour, I had lost fifty. Despite the weight loss, my deep tropical tan and Army dress uniform gave me a confident, healthy appearance.

The staff in Oakland consisted of civilians, primarily veterans, with a small military presence for validation and signature purposes.

Since most of us planned to leave the Army, the staff completed the out-processing quickly and efficiently. By the late afternoon of the first day, I had received my last Army paycheck, official discharge papers (DD-214), and an American Airlines ticket.

I caught a shuttle to Oakland Airport. I felt mixed emotions as I walked through the terminals—a strange brew of exhilaration and exhaustion. I was finally released from my service... and all I wanted to do was find a few weeks of quiet, solitude, and peace. I also felt nervous because I'd heard about the hostile reception of anti-war protesters toward returning veterans. After all, this was Northern California. San Francisco and the University of Berkeley, epicenters of Sixties radicalism, weren't far away.

Daily American life carried on around me, as carefree as I'd left it. People shuffled here and there, running to catch flights, buying magazines at newsstands, reading the signs for their flight times. Few people noticed me or paid attention. I felt relief that nobody became rude or aggressive... but everyone preoccupied themselves with life as they knew it; they remained oblivious and indifferent. I don't know what I should have expected, but I remembered where I'd been just seventy-two hours earlier. It seemed like I "straddled" a gap between two separate worlds that didn't reconcile easily.

One thing hadn't changed... I was hungry! I had an intense craving for an American cheeseburger and a large order of fries. I entered one of the airport's lounges, and everyone seated there looked at me in my uniform. I paused for a moment, unsure of what to do next. But then, the bartender welcomed me home and offered to make me whatever I wanted, free of charge. That put me at ease. He had probably seen this scene a thousand times since Vietnam began.

The bartender's generosity reminded me that not everyone had lost their minds over the Vietnam War. Perhaps he'd seen enough of us pass through to know how we carried the emotional weight of our experiences long after leaving the battlefield, but he offered the kindest thing he could have done at that moment. Even if you disagree with the premise of a war, I think it's important to acknowledge the bravery and self-sacrifice of military personnel. Somebody has to do the work of protecting and defending freedom; it doesn't "just happen." Next time you see them, do something kind for our men and women in uniform. That meal was the best I'd had in a year.

I returned home to a warm, loving gathering of family and friends. We enjoyed delicious Southern cuisine and had a delightful time together. I spent several days reflecting, walking, sitting, and simply *breathing*. I was nineteen years old, but somehow, I felt much older. I found joy simply through sitting still on my parent's front porch, watching the fireflies, and hearing the crickets chirp at dusk. The last thing I wanted was to go out and "raise hell," as many young men do. It felt good to be home.

A few weeks later, I packed up my belongings and made my way to East Tennessee. I'd been accepted to Lee College (now known as Lee University) in a town called Cleveland, east of Chattanooga.

Life Goes On

The average annual enrollment at Lee College was 1,200 students. After 1971, it increased significantly, averaging from 2,000 to 2,500 students. The sudden spike came from guys like me—returning Vietnam veterans taking advantage of the Montgomery GI Bill education benefit.

From 1965 to 1970, enrollment at college and university campuses skyrocketed from young men avoiding the draft. The trend continued after 1973, as approximately half of the country's sixteen million veterans pursued higher education or vocational training. The GI Bill covered tuition, books, supplies, counseling services, and a living allowance, leading to a massive surge in postwar college and vocational school attendance. This also prevented millions of veterans from flooding the job market all at once. By working part-time, I extended it beyond college and covered most of the costs of my graduate degree.

I wasn't a good student in high school, but serving in Vietnam changed my outlook on higher education. Though the traditional classroom setting was challenging, I now had an unquenchable thirst for knowledge, a broader understanding of the world around me, and complete confidence that if I applied myself, I would succeed. How hard could it be compared to dodging bullets while rescuing destroyed vehicles in a sweaty jungle? My first spring at Lee was wonderful, surrounded by the sweet scent of blooming dogwoods, redbuds, and shade blossoms dotting the campus. The only booby traps I had to worry about were my final exams.

The New Battlefront

Returning Vietnam veterans with combat and operational stress reactions or combat stress injury (a condition that was undiagnosed at the time) frequently found work or college overwhelming. I know I did. Many of my veteran peers dropped out of college after the first semester.

To casual observers, most of the impact of war is invisible; it's spiritual and psychological rather than physical (unless you have a noticeable injury). After the initial excitement of returning home wore off, I often felt overwhelmed by grief, anxiety, and inexplicable sadness... and I couldn't figure out why. Productive activities like jogging or playing sports helped me cope. They kept me busy and stopped me from dwelling too much on my experiences in Vietnam. They helped me manage my emotions until I felt better. I fought off grief this way for a long time, and it was enough to keep me going through college.

During my first semester at Lee, I joined a campus ministry group that consisted mainly of Vietnam veterans. Because many of us had similar experiences during the war, it helped me quickly readjust to a post-Vietnam environment and form close relationships. The group had a very active presence on campus, and we often had lively conversations, especially when discussing worldviews. Our insights as veterans were different from those of typical first-year college students, so our professors treated us differently. They recognized and appreciated our unique perspective, which helped to enrich the classroom environment.

As I finished my sophomore year, I began to sense God calling me to enter ministry. I wasn't sure which path to take: pastoral work, youth work, missions, education, or institutional chaplaincy. It was time to declare my major, so I decided to pursue Biblical Education as my primary and minor in History. Military recruiters frequently visited our campus looking for graduates interested in becoming officers. Some of my friends suggested I would make an excellent military chaplain. I had never considered that; grateful as I was for my experience as a soldier, I had no interest in returning to active duty.

The Call Goes Out

The spring semester of my junior year came, and I still had uncertainty about my plans after graduation. Then, some friends invited me to a camp meeting in Chattanooga, where prominent pastors, teachers, and speakers discussed various issues of the post-Vietnam culture. One of the speakers was Major Bob Crick, an Army chaplain who had served two tours in Vietnam. One of those tours was with the 173rd Airborne Brigade—the same unit Lynn West had served with during his first combat tour. Bob recounted a story about his closest friend, Major Charlie Waters, who died protecting wounded soldiers from enemy fire during the battle of Dak To in 1967. Waters was posthumously awarded the Congressional Medal of Honor for his actions that day.

Chaplain Crick ended his presentation with a second story about a Green Beret captain he met at the Army's Basic Airborne Course at Fort Benning, GA. The man had been raised in a Christian household but had strayed from his upbringing. When Bob suggested he participate in the worship service at the airborne chapel that Sunday, the captain scoffed at the idea, saying he had better things to do. But at the end of the service, when Bob finished his sermon and invited the congregation to the altar to pray, that same young officer was among the first to step forward.

Bob developed a strong friendship with that young captain. He brought his family, and they became active participants in the chapel program. Sadly, the captain had to leave for Vietnam, where he died while helping evacuate other soldiers from a firebase under attack by the enemy. The story had a tragic ending, but it was tinged with the hope of heaven. Except for Bob's intervention, he might have gone to his death without a relationship with God.

Bob's story stayed with me throughout the afternoon, as though God was trying to convey a message through it. I couldn't figure out why my heart felt so burdened, so I went off to pray alone. I spent time asking the Lord to help me understand the heavy-heartedness and what it all meant. After praying, I sat quietly and waited in a long silence. And then, He spoke to my heart, asking if I was willing to become a military chaplain for Him—even though it wasn't part of my plan.

I began making excuses, like Moses at the burning bush. But none of them held water, and I couldn't ignore what I felt I was being asked to do. I said, "Here I am, Lord. Send me!" I embraced my calling to be a chaplain, just as I had accepted my role as a soldier during the early weeks of Army Basic Training.

I planned to return to active duty as an Army chaplain and applied for a direct commission as an officer in the Army Reserve. As a part of the application process, the Army had to retrieve my 201 File (Official Military Record), which I had surrendered in Oakland. A significant issue during the Vietnam War was inadequate maintenance of military records, primarily due to personnel turnover or indifference, and my 201 File contained missing information they needed to process my application. Fortunately, I had kept copies of award certificates and other significant documents from my time in Vietnam. Even so, a process that should have taken six months took much longer because someone, somewhere, didn't do their job. (That happens from time to time in the military.)

I finished my studies at Lee and enrolled in Southwestern Baptist Theological Seminary in Fort Worth, Texas. The Army approved my application for a Reserve commission during my first semester. The seminary chaplain, a retired Army colonel, organized a small ceremony to administer the Oath of Office, and I was pinned as one of the Army's newest second lieutenants. My parents brimmed with pride. It was the first step in many milestones of my military career, and all because I trusted the Lord and seized the opportunities He set before me.

The Army flew me to New York that summer, to the peaceful setting of Fort Wadsworth on Staten Island's eastern shore, near the Verrazano-Narrows Bridge. There, I spent six weeks learning basic skills to become an Army officer and chaplain. Anyone could wander through the accessible base without prior notice as if it were just another neighborhood in the city. Across the bridge were Long Island and Brooklyn, and if you looked north on a clear day, you could see the Statue of Liberty with the Manhattan Skyline in the background. To a simple Southern boy from rural Tennessee, places like New York City felt just as foreign as Vietnam!

Shaping and Being Shaped

After returning to Fort Worth, I was offered a job as a special staff officer for the 2nd Brigade, 49th Armored Division, a Texas National Guard unit near the seminary campus. I knew transitioning from an enlisted soldier to a respected officer required more than a six-week course, so I was eager to learn from the unit's more experienced leaders. Unfortunately, none of the company commanders in the brigade had served in Vietnam. In some ways, I had more hands-on experience operating around heavy tanks than they did. Despite this, I readily accepted any opportunity to gain more experience in my new role as an Army officer.

After the fall of Saigon in 1975, the Army downsized its operations. Some National Guard and Reserves volunteers were sent back to their respective parent units. This brought more soldiers into our brigade, including five Army captains who previously served as helicopter pilots in Vietnam. These five officers became my mentors, teaching me the ropes, which helped increase my visibility in the brigade. Typically, only local junior officers had a broader scope of influence. My ambition was to become a dependable and trustworthy leader for my superiors and an example subordinates would willingly follow.

After finishing seminary, I returned home to Tennessee, where I became the pastor of a rural church in the small town of Woodbury, some twenty miles southeast of Murfreesboro. At the time, Woodbury was primarily known for producing bootleg moonshine whisky. The people of the church were extremely kind-hearted, generous, and very good to me. The small congregation of about fifty members included schoolteachers, construction workers, small business owners, and retirees. To supplement my income, I worked as a substitute teacher in the local school system.

False Alarm

I'd served at the Woodbury church for less than a year when I received a call from a much larger church in Baltimore, Maryland. They were searching for a first associate pastor, and someone recommended me. This church requested an interview as soon as possible. I received an unexpected opportunity that rarely presented itself so early in a minister's career.

I traveled to Baltimore, and during my time there, the senior pastor, his wife, and their family treated me like a VIP. They introduced me to several church members, some of their closest friends, and the principal leaders of the congregation. All the attention I received indicated that my interview had gone well, and I felt flattered. I delivered my Sunday sermon in my usual Southern drawl, and surprisingly, it resonated with the audience. Later, I learned that many members originated from the South.

As wonderful as the experience in Baltimore had been, I resolved to tread cautiously, assess carefully, and seek guidance from the Lord before making decisions. An offer came within a couple of weeks, but I still hadn't received a green light, so I asked for more time to think it over. More weeks passed, and the Baltimore church grew anxious. I was determined to wait until I had a definite answer, but even when I prayed three times a day, I still didn't hear anything. So, I surrendered the matter and went back to doing what I'd always done, which was to concentrate on the needs of the community. I told God I would remain in Woodbury if He desired that for me. I had matured when you consider how I'd responded at Fort Rucker when the Army changed my MOS. I was in a state of complete surrender.

True Alarm

Then, one day, I received a call from my chaplain commission offering me the opportunity to return to active duty immediately. Usually, returning to active duty required two years of practical experience, but the commission was willing to waive the requirement. However, they stipulated that I would have to switch military branches to accept the offer. The position was in the U.S. Navy.

I had mixed feelings of excitement and disappointment. I was comfortable in the Army and knew how to navigate their system with ease. The Navy meant uncharted waters, both literally and figuratively. When I'd listened to Bob Crick give his testimony and prayed for direction, everything in my imagination pointed toward wearing Army green. I didn't grow up as a seafaring man on boats by the oceanfront, and I anticipated a big learning curve. Although the Army and the Navy serve the same country and salute each other's officers, they have distinctive cultures and slang that take time to learn. The branches also poke fun at each other. (In that area I was an expert; just a short time before the opportunity came up, I'd been joking about the Navy with a few soldier friends. Now, if I accepted, I would have to eat my words.)

On the other hand, I saw plenty of upside. The Navy would accept me directly as an officer, which meant I did not need to undergo their basic training or spend more time going through "A" School, their version of Advanced Individual Training. I'd also volunteered for enough missions and crazy jobs in Vietnam to know this: you never know what you'll miss out on if you stay in your comfort zone! The Navy would take me to some interesting places on the map, and active-duty life would present the challenge I had longed for and missed since leaving Vietnam. Full-time military service would bring back some of the camaraderie and brotherly devotion I'd struggled to find in civilian employment.

That night, I prayed and gave thanks to the Lord for everything He'd done for me. I felt so grateful for the people of Woodbury. I loved my congregation, the community, and all the challenges that came with loving people who felt underappreciated or insignificant. Through them, God enlarged my heart, crowding out the selfishness and replacing it with compassion for others. The Lord spoke to my heart and said, "I know you're disappointed about the Navy, but would you go for Me?" I responded the only way I could: "Yes, Lord, send me!"

So, in April 1980, off I went to the Basic Navy Chaplains Course at the Naval Education and Training Center (NETC) in Newport, Rhode Island. After I completed the training, I received my first assignment: squadron chaplain for the commander of Destroyer Squadron Twenty-Three in San Diego, California.

Anchors Aweigh

The earth's oceans have a few common qualities—beauty, vastness, and unpredictability. We know the oceans can only come so far before land rises above them, offering stability. It takes just one look to see their beauty and vastness. If you've ever swum far out enough from the beach or through waves, you know the chaos and power of the waters. For me, they served as a great physical reminder of the spiritual journey I embarked on.

In hindsight, God's offer of a career in the Navy aligned with the life He appointed for me. If I wanted to play it safe and try to hang onto my illusion of control, I could have stayed on land. But I was made for more than that, and I'd been tested and molded already. As John Shedd once said, "A ship is safe in harbor, but that's not what ships are for." Even at such a young age, I'd experienced too many close calls and crazy adventures in Vietnam to keep fearing the unknown. If you think you've reached the limit of following God, you can rest assured—there is more ahead!

My new role in the U.S. Navy became the perfect opportunity to set sail in search of more of the treasure I'd found by trusting Him in the first place: the Hope of War.

My good friend Captain David Howard, later promoted to Colonel (O-6), and I on our graduation day from Army Chaplain School at Fort Wadsworth on Staten Island, New York, summer 1975. After graduation, David became an Airborne Ranger, among many other things. Unfortunately, he passed away on active duty due to an undiagnosed heart condition. His ministry was very impactful; everyone who knew him mourned his loss.

My first official picture as a Navy Chaplain for Destroyer Squadron Twenty-Three, homeported at 32nd Street Naval Base in San Diego, CA. June 1980.

Rear Admiral James Walley, Jr., Deputy Chief of Civil Engineers, Naval Facilities Engineering Command, Washington, D.C., presents me with the Defense Meritorious Service Medal at an awards ceremony held at the Washington Navy Shipyard, May 2002. The ceremony recognized me as one of the senior watch officers who coordinated ministry and pastoral support following the 9/11 terrorist attack on the Pentagon.

The photo from a public relations article that covered my work at Destroyer Squadron Twenty-Three from 1980 to 1982. During this time, I introduced a unique approach to ministry designed explicitly for destroyers and frigates. The success of this program led Commander Navy Surface Force Pacific to publicize it across the entire fleet as an example of how spiritual preparedness impacts combat readiness.

Receiving an award for contributing to post-conflict stabilization efforts in Bosnia and Herzegovina in 1997. I served in Stabilization Force (SFOR), a NATO-led multinational peacekeeping force deployed to the former Yugoslavia following the Bosnian War. During my service in NATO, I became the Command Chaplain for the Joint Civil Multinational Task Force (JCMTF), comprised of 19 allied nations.

General Eric Shinseki, who later served as the 34th U.S. Army Chief of Staff until his retirement, commanded the allied coalition. At the time Shinseki also held the positions of Commanding General of the Seventh United States Army, Commander of Allied Land Forces Central Europe, and Commander of NATO Stabilization Force in Bosnia and Herzegovina.

My official command photo during service as the Division Chaplain/
Assistant Chief of Staff for Religious Ministry in the 4th Marine
Division, Fleet Marine Force, Marine Forces Reserve, New Orleans,
LA, 2003-08. I held this position during Operation Iraqi Freedom
(OIF), which included first and second combat offensives in Fallujah.

An award ceremony at the Navy Expeditionary Combat Command
(NECC) in Joint Expeditionary Base Little Creek–Fort Story, Virginia
Beach, VA. NECC provides expeditionary capabilities in some of the
most remote, complex, and austere environments worldwide. That day,
I received the Legion of Merit (Gold Star indicating second award) for
my leadership as NECC's Force Family Readiness Director. The
recognition meant a lot, and I was proud to be surrounded by my
colleagues and peers who supported me throughout my tour. Together,
we oversaw programs to help sailors and their families build resiliency
necessary to face repeated deployments in support of Operation Iraqi
Freedom (OIF) and Operation Enduring Freedom (OEF) in
Afghanistan. NECC thoughtfully presented my wife, Charlene, with a
certificate of appreciation for her continual support of my ministry.

Chapter Twelve
From Unfinished Business to Freedom

Every human life is "a work in progress." If we walked around with that idea stamped on our foreheads, we might avoid some of the spiritual "holes" we dig. I thought the passage of time would bring closure to Vietnam and the bumpy road of transition... but I was wrong.

I began my naval career as a chaplain in the spring of 1980, as Ronald Reagan started his campaign to become the 40th President of the United States. Reagan believed Americans had lost faith in themselves and their national destiny. Between the failure in Vietnam, President Richard Nixon's resignation, the fallout from the Watergate scandal, and the mistakes of incumbent President Jimmy Carter... things looked bleak. Reagan's speeches and writings emphasized the importance of recapturing the "lost vision of our founding fathers."[1]

Reagan introduced two major political reforms to restore America's confidence. The first stimulated the American economy through deregulation, reduced federal spending, and across-the-board tax cuts. The second outlined a "Peace Through Strength" foreign policy to end the Cold War—by winning it. Once in office, Reagan had the necessary sway to accomplish these objectives—the power of the presidency and his innate ability as a truly great communicator.[2]

Some belligerent foreign powers seemed to understand the new president better than Congress or the media. On the day of Reagan's inauguration in 1981, the fundamentalist leaders of the Iranian Revolution released all fifty-two American hostages they'd held for the previous 444 days during the Carter presidency rather than face the consequences. In 1986, after sponsoring the bombing of a West Berlin discotheque frequented by U.S. troops, Libyan leader Moammar Qaddafi ran and hid after Reagan ordered airstrikes on Tripoli.

Reagan rejected the "Vietnam syndrome"—the idea that Americans were unwilling to support military action because of the

Vietnam War. He took the Soviet and communist threats seriously, and believed the U.S. alone possessed the wealth, power, obligation, and moral authority to defeat them. Many of Reagan's speeches aimed to remind Americans of their identity as bold, determined, and free people who played a critical role in overcoming the forces of tyranny.[3] As the ancient Latin proverb goes, "Si vis pacem para bellum." Translated, it means, "If you want peace, prepare for war."

Restoring the Foundations

To address the country's economic woes, Reagan presented a series of corrective actions to re-energize the American industrial sector, reduce government spending, and decrease the tax burden citizens faced (at the time, the highest marginal tax rate was seventy percent). These proposals resonated with the American people, leading them to embrace a renewed sense of patriotism and perseverance. By the late 1980s, the top marginal rate had been slashed from seventy percent to twenty-eight percent. Inflation fell dramatically, home ownership soared, and American lifestyle and upward mobility standards improved by leaps and bounds.

Reagan believed the federal government was responsible for the country's loss of confidence and economic capability. Like Nixon, he addressed the American people directly and emphasized the federal government's role in the nation's affairs in line with the Founders' vision. These were not impromptu political statements; he developed these beliefs over decades of fighting communism in Hollywood and campaigning for conservative candidates and causes. They carried forward into his two terms as governor of California and his presidential candidacies in 1968 and 1976.

Life in America felt palpably different as Reagan handed the reins to his successor, Vice President George H.W. Bush, in 1989. We enjoyed six years of uninterrupted, exponential economic growth and made enormous strides in technology, medicine, and standard of living. Abroad, we became dominant against the Soviet menace.

Mikhail Gorbachev, the last Soviet leader, openly admitted to the shortcomings of Marxism-Leninism and the pointlessness of Russian imperialism. Less than two years after Reagan's departure, the Berlin Wall fell, signaling the permanent collapse of the Soviet Union onto the ash heap of history. As British Prime Minister Margaret Thatcher put it, Reagan ended the Cold War "without firing a shot."[4]

Water Damage

Between unclear policies from the Carter White House and reduced funding from Congress, the U.S. Navy struggled in 1980 to compete with its Soviet counterpart. Although the United States had more aircraft carriers (twenty-one to Russia's three), the Soviets had more surface warships (443 to 196) and submarines (294 to 119). The alignment of naval and national strategy needed a makeover, with consensus on the Navy's primary mission and how fleets should be structured to achieve it.[5]

The Carter Administration supported the NATO strategy, which used most of America's military resources to assist the Allied front in Europe. That made the Navy responsible for safeguarding the Atlantic Ocean's sea lines of communication (SLOC), which required only a few multiple large-deck carriers. However, the SLOC strategy raised concerns among Navy leaders, such as Admiral James Holloway, Chief of Naval Operations. They believed this policy made other critical wartime duties impossible. It also yielded the Pacific, the largest theater, to the Soviets.[6]

Reagan chose John Lehman as Secretary of the Navy. Lehman introduced an aggressive plan for renewal, growing the Navy to the size and strength it could defeat the combined Warsaw Pact navies and destroy Soviet strategic assets using carrier-based air power. What an exciting time to be a sailor, especially as a U.S. Navy pilot! Millions of young Americans were drawn to naval careers in the 1980s by popular movies like *Top Gun*, showcasing the resurgence of American naval prowess and the importance of remaining vigilant against evil forces threatening freedom.

Under Lehman's leadership, the Navy nearly doubled its size and vastly improved its efficiency and technological superiority.[7] Advanced technologies, such as precision-guided munitions, electronic warfare, and standoff jamming capabilities, became commonplace and propelled a renaissance of U.S. maritime dominance. The United States faced multiple global threats aside from the Soviet Union. Still, the Navy had enough ships to manage the Middle East and the Caribbean, *as well as* execute demonstrations in the Pacific and Atlantic.

In 1983, when Marxists overthrew Grenada's democratic government, the United States intervened with twelve warships, including a carrier.[8] Three years later, the Navy mobilized three carriers and twenty-three other warships to Libya to challenge Gaddafi's excessive claims in the Gulf of Sidra.[9] During the Iran-Iraq Tanker War, the Navy successfully escorted 270 tankers in 135 convoys in the Persian Gulf, thwarting Iran's efforts to intimidate Iraq's Arab supporters and ensure the flow of oil from the Gulf.[10]

Larry the Landlubber

Destroyer Squadron Twenty-Three (DESRON-23) is homeported at Naval Base San Diego in California, also known as the "32nd Street Naval Station." The base is situated near the eastern end of the Coronado Bridge, which spans picturesque San Diego Bay, connecting San Diego to Coronado Island.

I felt overwhelmed when I arrived. I had an "out of the frying pan, into the fire" sensation in the pit of my stomach. Joining DESRON-23 was an incredible opportunity for a newly graduated Navy lieutenant, but truthfully, I felt conflicted. I was a brand-new sailor with no naval experience, serving in a highly decorated naval command during years of peak tension between two nuclear-armed global superpowers. You could call it a "redux" of how I felt when I learned of my assignment to the 11th Armored Cavalry Regiment in Camp Di An... I felt *way* out of my league.

I requested an assignment to a Marine battalion. Marines are organized similarly to the Army, with divisions, regiments, battalions, and companies. However, the assigning officer disagreed; after reviewing my record, he believed the best thing for me was to gain exposure to the Navy's mindset and standard procedures. By now, I should have expected to be thrown into the deep end, with God involved—head-first, with little to no idea of what lay in store. When we don't know how to do something, God prefers the traditional, fatherly way of teaching children to swim: "Throw 'em in and let 'em learn." He knows we learn more from pain and frustration than we do sitting in the classroom.

The squadron I joined had five destroyers and frigates, with the primary mission of protecting and escorting carrier battle groups. As the least experienced officer on the commodore's staff, I wanted to demonstrate that I could contribute to combat readiness. I had no idea how to minister to a destroyer squadron. However, I could see the similarities to working as a circuit rider—you traveled from one congregation to another, teaching groups and counseling individual officers and sailors. The only difference was that my "circuit" consisted of five navy ships or, during extended deployments, any ship in the battle group that required chaplain support.

My uniform's Army combat ribbons made me stick out like a sore thumb, but they also gave me advantages. They piqued sailors' interest, which led to lengthy conversations, particularly about my experience in Vietnam. Through these casual conversations, I established strong relationships with commanding officers, which helped me gain support from their wardroom officers, chiefs, and crews.

What To Do with a Drunken Sailor?

In the 1980s, the typical ship deployment schedule was one year in port, followed by six months at sea. Long months at sea in various weather conditions caused significant wear and tear, both on the ships and the crews who operated them. But if you think six months at sea is hard, try being on land! While in port, the ships went to nearby shipyards for refurbishment before the next deployment. Then we did "sea trials" and "pre-deployment workups." We worked long days and nights, year-round, regardless of weather or conditions.

Then, we had the issue of the sailors themselves. During the post-Vietnam era, the all-volunteer Navy didn't live up to the expectations set by officials in Washington. After the government abolished the draft, the Navy had to compete with the civilian labor market to fill its ranks. As a result, manpower policy shifted towards a free-market model. This meant that for most prospective sailors, the primary incentives for joining were structure, discipline, and enlistment bonuses.

During the Carter years, the Navy's budget shrank substantially, and it relaxed its approach toward substance abuse and behavioral issues. Shriveled budgets led to a lack of enlistment incentives, while leniency led to low discipline, morale, and performance. Many junior officers and seasoned NCOs—the backbone of the Navy—left active duty. Many potential recruits saw little to no benefit in signing up.

The Reagan Administration reversed course, reinstituting and enforcing a "zero tolerance" policy towards substance abuse and discipline-related issues. It improved performance, quality of life, and retention of the Navy's best personnel. The surge in military spending during Reagan's first term created a slew of bonuses and incentives for prospective officers and enlisted sailors. For young people across the country, naval service suddenly became a viable career choice again.

For most of 1981 and 1982, my day-to-day life dealt with the consequences of young sailors' poor choices while the new tone took effect. It left little time for creative or proactive ministry, which could have gone a long way to reduce or prevent behavioral problems.

After a year of work, I began feeling emotionally and spiritually exhausted. I regretted leaving the Army for the Navy. It felt like too much for one person; I needed to "duplicate myself" and form a ministry *team* that could function with or without my presence. The squadron had many dedicated lay leaders, but they needed training and resources to establish a sustainable ministry for each ship. Something had to be done to improve the spiritual atmosphere; too much lay at stake if we ignored it.

Diligent Hands Bring Wealth

One day, during a monthly chaplains' meeting at the Naval Air Station North Island, the senior chaplain explained his struggle to manage the base chapel programs with such limited funds. Generally, operations consumed the commander's budget, and chapel programs received whatever was left over. He said the situation changed once he started using the Navy's new Planning, Programming, Budgeting, and Execution (PPBE) process.

No one had ever attempted PPBE for a destroyer squadron before, but as soon as I learned of it, I could tell it would solve many of our problems. Every Navy commander understands PPBE. It simplifies decision-making and takes the "guesswork" out of planning. DESRON-23 would soon undergo a change of squadron leadership, so I dedicated several weeks to studying and organizing plans, programs, and budgets to showcase the ministry's ability to improve the squadron's combat readiness.

I finished work on an outline a few days before the new commodore, Captain Tom Jacobs, arrived at the squadron. He came from Washington, D.C., where he'd worked for the Chief of Naval

Operations. During staff interviews, Jacobs expressed his low opinion of chaplains. He believed they occupied space on the staff that could be put to better use. He didn't understand how chaplains spent their time or how to measure their impact.

I couldn't exactly blame him; Jacobs had spent the previous few years working under the conditions of the Carter Administration, with its anemic military spending and disregard for morale among the armed services. He'd been around long enough to know how often politicians required the military to squeeze out productivity, effort, and victory... without financial or moral support. I would have felt the same way, knowing the importance of his mission.

I also agreed with his skepticism about the return on investment. How can you possibly know if a chaplain's ministry genuinely impacts the command mission when you can't produce evidence or numbers? When I worked for my dad building houses in Smithville, he *always* counted the costs and measured carefully before signing contracts or accepting a customer's money. Even when you're neck-deep building a house, you still "measure twice and cut once." I organized my life and my ministry this way, too: "Waste not, want not."

Government spending frequently lacks accountability or consequences, while wisely managing personal money requires you to account for every penny. Jacobs raised the objections I hoped he would. He wanted detailed plans and timely, measurable results if he had to spend money on a command ministry program. I wanted those, too, and it took him by surprise when I presented my PPBE plan for his review. The last thing he expected was a well-prepared response, giving him the precise data and financial projections he wanted!

After his review, Jacobs asked me to prepare a brief for the squadron commander's entire leadership team. Things continued to improve when the Commander of the Pacific Fleet's staff chaplain learned what I'd done and supported its broader implementation. To cut a long story short, the Command Religious Program became a model for ministry in the fleet. It took ministry aboard destroyer squadrons from a vague, transcendent concept into a practical, measurable one. As the old saying goes, "Don't be so heavenly-minded that you're no earthly good." Help people make good decisions based on facts and data, and you'll earn their trust.

DESRON-23 shaped how I handled every subsequent assignment for the rest of my career. With each new mission, I added to that foundation, building a track record and reputation for leading military ministry in a meaningful, measurable way. I earned the trust of senior leaders and served at the highest levels of command by adapting to and serving their needs and helping ensure their success.

Redeeming the Foundation

As much as God wants us to be preoccupied with serving our fellow man, I believe He is equally, deeply concerned about our spiritual condition—especially if we've taken on a spiritual "sickness" that hasn't fully healed, restored, or reintegrated. I spent the next two decades faithfully serving my fellow sailors, but I had work to do in my own soul, and I remained unaware. By keeping myself busy serving others, these deeper issues festered. So, God had to force me to come to the spiritual operating table.

When I built homes with my dad, I learned to be mindful of things that hide beneath the floors and behind the walls. Pests, mold, rust, and water damage from burst pipes have the potential to destroy large sections of a home, and homeowners don't usually realize they have a problem until it's too late. In the same way, God will shake us out of our false sense of security and force us to confront our past so we can grow into our future.

But sometimes, you go through hell before you get to bring heaven to earth.

The Wake-Up Call Heard Around the World

My family and I lived in North Carolina when Islamic terrorists attacked America on September 11, 2001. We watched in horror as the events of the day unfolded. That evening, my command chaplain told me to report to the Navy Chief of Chaplains Office at the Navy Annex in Arlington, Virginia. I made my way there the following day, approaching from the Maryland side of the District of Columbia. I passed the Pentagon, where thick black smoke still emanated from the building.

Suddenly, I had a queasy feeling in the pit of my stomach and felt woefully unprepared for what lay ahead. I remembered how war changes everything and impacts everyone it touches. Aware of my weakness, I whispered a prayer, asking the Lord for wisdom and guidance. He reminded me of David, who became king but started with little besides hope and potential. Through multiple encounters with dangerous wild animals, David discovered that God's strength is sufficient for any threat—even a giant of a man like Goliath. And we had just absorbed a Goliath-level attack!

I reported to the Navy Annex and immediately assisted one of the Casualty Assistance Calls Officers (CACOs). They notify families of injuries, deaths, or missing personnel. We got started right away; an hour later, we approached our first house in Alexandria, Virginia. There, we met the wife of a missing Navy commander who'd been at his new job in the Pentagon for only two weeks when the attacks occurred. They were expecting their first child. Sadly, we had no good news for her, except that the rescue teams at the Pentagon crash site were doing everything possible to locate him. We had many sad stops that day.

For three weeks after the Pentagon attack, I worked various shifts at the Navy Annex and stood watch in the evenings at the chaplain's tent near the crash site. I offered spiritual guidance to anyone who asked, including people who rarely or never visited the chaplain's office. War has a way of changing people's perspectives, making them more reflective about their lives and where they stand with the Lord. It humbled and moved me to offer comfort and support during such a trying time.

I visited survivors in hospitals and listened to their stories. Some shared how they navigated through heat, smoke, and darkness to find an exit point. Others talked about being buried under mountains of debris and led to safety by a stranger's reassuring voice. Some sounded as though they'd passed surreally from one reality to another. One minute, they stood talking to friends and coworkers; the next, they woke up in hospital beds, learning they were the lone survivors in their office.

One of them asked me, "Chaplain, why did I survive while my friends perished?" That question gripped me so profoundly that I didn't know what to say.

The Lingering Question

In the weeks after returning home from the Pentagon, I spent many nights wrestling with intense grief and anxiety. I lost my appetite and dropped twenty pounds in two weeks. Bewildered, I couldn't move beyond the emotional struggle. I couldn't sleep at night, and that survivor's question played repeatedly in my head:

"Why did I survive while my friends perished?"

I needed to talk with someone, to try to isolate whatever was eating me alive. I made an appointment to visit an old friend, an Army chaplain at Fort Bragg in North Carolina. We spent an hour or more discussing the Pentagon. We talked about visiting the bereaved family members and praying for the maimed survivors lying in hospital beds. I'm familiar with sadness and intensity. I'm accustomed to sights like the carnage and wreckage at the Pentagon, which might keep some people up at night … but not me. In the years between Vietnam and

9/11, I'd witnessed plenty of brokenness and trauma—the saddest parts of being a ministry leader.

But *something* gnawed away at me. My friend asked me to look back on my own history, specifically about my time in Vietnam.

"That was a long time ago," I replied. "There's nothing to discuss. We talked a while longer. Then, my friend asked again: "Why don't you tell me about Vietnam?" But I ignored the question and tried to change the subject.

That was my "tell." He nailed me for sidestepping Vietnam. Ironically, the same guy who never dodged the draft, didn't hide in the National Guard, and never applied for a deferment to avoid service in Vietnam... the same guy who went willingly and became hooked on the adventures he had there... *that* same guy, now wanted to run and hide to avoid any discussion of Vietnam.

"Larry," he said, "you don't have to talk about gory details. Just tell me how your time in Vietnam impacted you."

And then it came. The response went off like a bomb in my soul and flew out of my mouth before I could stop it. My heart exploded in my chest, my voice kicked up with intensity, and I let him feel the weight of what ate me up inside.

"I'll tell you how it impacted me," I snapped. "I feel guilty! *Guilty* for surviving the war and living a great life when so many others were deprived of the opportunity!"

Now I knew why that survivor's question hit me like a ton of bricks! I'd nursed survivor's guilt for over thirty years. I was back at Firebase Ham Tan, watching my close friends die just days before they were due to go home and sneaking off into a secluded jungle space to sob until I drained my soul of its grief. My eyes flooded with tears of sorrow... yet when I opened them, I saw no jungle, rice paddies, or napalm-filled explosions. I only saw my friend's kind, patient eyes, silently bearing witness to the collapse of a spiritual wall I should never have built.

More floodgates of tears opened on my drive home… but they opened to *light*. For the first time in three decades, I finally understood the meaning of what I'd been through in Vietnam. God spoke to my heart during that drive. He told me how, by guarding my emotional wounds for years, I had prevented Him from using them for His purposes. He showed me how my past had everything to do with my future. I felt a little like Simon Peter, the apostle, as the Lord "poked the bear" a little more through a series of three questions he asked me:

Will you acknowledge that you are prone to grief, just like everyone else?

Will you entrust your wounded heart to me, let me heal your pain, and use it to assist others facing the challenges ahead?

Will you confront issues like this in faith instead of hiding or suppressing them?

I responded the only way I could: "Yes, Lord, I confess. I'm no different from anyone else. I acknowledge my weaknesses and dishonesty, especially in my spiritual journey with You. And I won't hide my pain and grief anymore; I will let You use them however You think best." Then, at last, came a massive sense of relief as the grip of guilt and sorrow over my life began to loosen. I felt *alive*–more than I had in years! My appetite came back, the depression lifted, and I could function again.

Over the years, grief resurfaced from time to time. I learned to make a conscious effort to surrender the situation to the Holy Spirit, my "air support." If necessary, I call in "ground forces" by talking through the pain some more with other men I trust. As evangelical pastor Jack Hayford said, "What lives in the darkness dies in the light." If we conceal or suppress our darkness, it gathers strength. But with the light of God and like-hearted others, you can gain "fire superiority" over it.

Turn the "Mess" Into a "Message"

From my own readjustment struggles after returning from Vietnam, I spent the final decade of my military career helping to develop programs to equip people to fight back against destruction from within. I taught veterans, family members, and community leaders the signs and symptoms of struggle and how to seek additional support or professional help. People often attach stigmas to warriors looking for help when they feel torn apart by the horrors of war and the burdens of serving in combat. I taught forcefully against that and discouraged people from paying any attention to those stigmas.

By far, the most challenging battle most service members face is to "let go" of their identity as warriors once they leave the combat zone. Many become caricatures of "angry war veterans," "disgruntled vets," and so forth. I appreciate the humor, but mostly, it's unfortunate; staying in "combat mode" after you leave combat isn't necessary. What's the point of putting your life on the line and making all those sacrifices only to spend the rest of your life angry and high-strung?

If you're fighting tooth and nail to overcome issues like this, don't give up or resign yourself to it! Find that presence, that "safe harbor" friend, who can listen and absorb the total weight of what you carry… without letting you stay there, weighed down by it. Go to God with all the anger and bitterness, and be honest about your feelings. He can handle your pain; His shoulders can take it. But whatever you do, don't keep silent and "stuff it down" in your soul. It won't go away just because you ignore it.

Surely, you can look back on decisions you made years or decades ago and see their formative role in who you are today. Will tomorrow be much different based on the decisions you make today? Do you still think, after what I've shared, that the destructive emotions you bring home from combat will just "vanish"?

And what if you've found peace and solace and dealt with your inner darkness? The answer is, "Don't keep the light to yourself!" Find someone else who served or is currently serving and be the light for them. Take your mess and turn it into a *message*!

I refuse to settle for sky-high rates of veteran homelessness, substance abuse, and suicide when there is so much we can do to prevent it. Let's catch more of our brothers and sisters before they fall. I do it all the time now, the same way someone helped me. I've never felt more humbled, satisfied, or rewarded than I do when I help a fellow warrior out of the pit of despair. As the apostle James wrote, "Whoever brings back a sinner from his wandering will save his soul from death and will cover over a multitude of sins."

And that, my friend, is *The Hope of War*!

Its been 23 years since Sept. 11, 2001, when terrorists turned four hijacked passenger jets into makeshift missiles that struck American soil. But the tragic day is still fresh in the minds of some of the Army's top leaders who survived the attack at the Pentagon. Positioned across the Potomac River from the nation's capital, the Pentagon is the nerve center for national defense. It's also one of the world's most significant office buildings, a workplace for roughly 23,000 military and civilian employees, including the Secretary of Defense and Chairman of the Joint Chiefs of Staff. The five-sided structure is a symbol of America's strength and security, which made it a target that September morning. The attack on the Pentagon killed all 64 people on board the aircraft and 125 people inside the Pentagon. In all, more than 2,977 people died during the Sept. 11 attacks, and more than 6,000 others were injured. Photos adapted from the public domain.

On January 4, 2020, my mom's younger brother, Charles "Roger" Underwood, passed away. Roger was a great mentor and helped me prepare for the challenges of my military career and professional ministry. He was an inspiring leader whose self-confidence and energy came from his spiritual roots and knowledge of the Scripture, which he applied as a partial owner of Distribution Construction Co. They specialized in building and installing natural gas pipeline distribution systems. Personal photograph from 2009.

In 2015, my brother Fred retired from his role as the owner and CEO of Distribution Construction Co. To celebrate this milestone, I joined him for a special occasion. Throughout my life, Fred and his wife, Barbara, have been a source of support, motivation, and inspiration. They are great friends and exceptional role models for our children and grandchildren.

Epilogue

Leaders rarely please the majority. Instead, they make tough decisions that align with the will of the Lord at the risk of upsetting the crowd. Spiritual and godly leaders act with confidence and conviction, even when they don't receive widespread approval. They do this because they know and understand information and circumstances the ordinary person doesn't want to face, and because they carefully consider the consequences of their actions.

This book is not, first and foremost, a complaint or criticism of Vietnam's political and military leaders. Their decisions and actions served as examples of a greater human reality: much of what we perceive as "news" or "history" is rarely the *whole* story. If we look beyond the media narrative (such as their spin on decisions by generals and presidents), we can recognize patterns that trickle down to our decision-making level as ordinary citizens. We can understand how our leaders are, in many ways, *reflections of us*. If we can read between the lines and realize what hampers them… maybe we can discern more about what hampers us.

In essence, I want to emphasize why truth and unchanging reality matter more than most people think and why it's so important to stand for them. One of Jesus' most famous sayings goes, "You shall know the truth, and the truth shall set you free." I hope you get more than the facts; I want you to know the *truth*. I don't mean "the hidden or redacted statements of certain politicians behind closed doors." What hope does that offer? The dark side of politics will never change. Instead, I'm talking about the truth about your military service or engagement in the process if you are non-military. I am referring to your tremendous sacrifice and the peace and security that free nations enjoy due to your willingness to risk your life for your country or a cause worth fighting for. Heroism, selflessness, and the bravery to give up one's life or self-interest for others have long-lasting effects. Such values go back to ancient times, representing the hope of war - which can only be achieved through faith, knowledge, commitment, and skill, no matter the circumstances.

Unfortunately, if you want to understand the truth, you must acknowledge and take responsibility for your role in it, even if it embarrasses you. I still remember the day President Richard Nixon resigned. More than anything, he lost credibility and support because he lied and attempted to cover up what he'd done. He may have received a pardon from his successor, but Nixon spent his remaining twenty years trying to regain his credibility, which proved even more difficult than trying to maintain it in the first place. We pay the price for dishonesty.

Now, Nixon couldn't have gotten off scot-free for coming clean about Watergate. Quite the opposite: both deceit and truth lead to consequences. But ask yourself this question: "What kind of consequences do you prefer?" One may preserve your body temporarily..., and the other preserves your soul forever. Which would you choose?

It depends on whether you can think long-term; many people refuse to. A lot of us could do with a look deeper into the past. We would benefit from a decision to stop swallowing the narrow-minded historical narrative of Vietnam and make up our own minds for a change.

We could also do with a brighter, broader future... and I believe The Hope of War is the path you take to get there.

History Versus the Past

Plenty of "history" is inaccurate. There's a difference between "the past" and "history." The past means "everything that happened," while history narrates certain events (and ignores others) from a particular point of view. The past, then, aligns more closely with the truth. The older I get, the less the present or the future surprises me. Because I study the past—the good, the bad, and the ugly – I often see the future coming before it arrives. Mark Twain once said, "History doesn't repeat itself, but it does rhyme."

When the United States military withdrew from South Vietnam, anti-war activists gained permanent, irreversible control over the war's historical narrative. Ever since then, they became adept at howling with feigned rage and despair whenever the U.S. deployed its military might. They spent most of the 1980s assailing President Ronald Reagan's anticommunist agenda. Another decade passed, and they fought tooth and nail against President George W. Bush's response to Islamic terror on 9/11. The pattern repeats itself, often because the anti-war left studies history, but they don't study the past. They have some of the facts… but not the whole truth.

Those anti-war activists ridiculed the idea that withdrawing from Vietnam would harm U.S. credibility or that the communists would turn vicious against the people they conquered. But what followed? Did our withdrawal pacify the communists or embolden them? Did they wreak greater havoc or not? The anti-war movement promised us that running away from Vietnam would restore our moral standing in the world and heal us as a nation. So why, just a few years later, did President Jimmy Carter take to the airwaves during primetime to lecture Americans about their "crisis of confidence"? By contrast, what made President Ronald Reagan's "national renewal" message so infectious that he defeated Carter in a landslide? Didn't the antiwar movement promise we would feel better about ourselves if we ran away? Why didn't it happen?

What about the Vietnamese people? Is it a mere coincidence that after the end of the Vietnam War, the U.S. absorbed enormous amounts of refugee immigrants from Southeast Asia? Perhaps as many as forty million people in Vietnam, Cambodia, and Laos perished under the brutal rule of communism. Six hundred thousand Vietnamese drowned in the South China Sea, attempting to defect and escape. Tens of thousands more were imprisoned in "reeducation" camps. When the U.S. withdrew its support from the anticommunist government of

Cambodia, seven million people lived there. Three years later, the Khmer Rouge had murdered or starved to death over two million of them. This is not to mention the plight of tens of millions of Southeast Asians who simply resigned themselves to living under communist rule.

Is that the history you hear about or see dramatized in movies about Vietnam? Personally, I see much more time devoted to satire and mockery of the young men I served with. The communists appear in these films as enemy troops, but we see little to no commentary or characterization of them; they escape judgment entirely. The main point of movies like *Platoon, Full Metal Jacket,* and *Apocalypse Now* was to discredit Vietnam veterans as primitive, cynical pawns who violated the warped morality of the Sixties anti-war movement... simply by saying "yes" when their nation called on them. Through their "yes," my brothers earned a lifetime of wrath from all those who said "no" to America's involvement in the war.

Yes, or No?

The truth and the past are simple. They're not *easy*, but they are simple, which makes them profound. When you look at the past, beyond the historical narratives of the media and the anti-war movement, you see Vietnam set us on a collision course with an eternal, unchanging truth: Every time you say "yes" to one thing, you say "no" to something else.

By saying "yes" to total victory in World War Two, the U.S. said "no" to an indefinite war, and millions of lives lost.

But by saying "no" to finishing the Soviet Union after they'd defeated the Nazis and the Japanese, the U.S. said "yes" to another 45 years of Cold War hostilities, which included Vietnam.

By saying "yes" to defending Europe and Asia from communism after World War Two, the U.S. said "no" to isolation and allowing tyrants to roam freely across the planet, threatening our security.

But by saying "yes" to the settlement between France and Indochina in 1954, the West said "no" to eradicating the communist threat in Vietnam. It was too late; we'd already said "yes" to the awkward position of negotiating with communist totalitarians in Russia and China. There wasn't going to be a peaceful outcome!

By saying "yes" to U.S. troops fighting the communists in Vietnam, we said "no" to the spread of communism in Southeast Asia.

But by saying "yes" to fighting an undeclared war with an undefined outcome, blindfolded and handcuffed by politics, and then constantly trying to escape responsibility and run away... our leaders said "no" to victory in Vietnam.

By saying "yes" to ending the war in Vietnam with honor... the U.S. said "no" to the "domino effect" Nixon had predicted since his time as vice president in the 1950s. When Congress changed that "yes" to a "no," Southeast Asia crumbled into communist hands, where it's remained ever since.

But by saying "yes" to treating communists as morally equivalent to the U.S., we said "no" to honoring the sacrifices our veterans made. We shamed and devalued the service of an entire generation of warriors. Regardless of what antiwar activists intended or whether they *thought* they merely sued for peace. They failed to think through what their actions would mean to the men who did the fighting.

Redeeming 'Nam

The good news is that by the same token, we can learn from and redeem the past. We can change what we say "yes" and "no" to.

By saying "yes" to my counselor friend when he pressed me about my time in Vietnam, I said "no" to hiding my pain and guilt. And when I'd healed and began to share my story, people's defenses lowered immediately. They sat stunned, paying close attention, when I opened my mouth and shared about what happened. I discovered the power of my stories to help the officers and leaders I mentored when it came to caring for warriors' well-being.

When Vietnam veterans returned home, they encountered indifference from the government and the Veterans Administration, as well as open cruelty and hostility from antiwar protesters. Their pleas for help with combat trauma went ignored. They found it difficult to reintegrate into society and transition back to civilian life. Homelessness and substance abuse among veterans skyrocketed and remain problematic through to the present day.

Despite evidence from America's previous wars about the devastating emotional and spiritual fallout from combat, senior leaders offered little, aside from empty promises, to help warriors readjust to everyday life. Warriors are trained to kill… but they're not taught how to cope with the aftermath. I'd already experienced reintegration; I knew how long it could take for a veteran to detach themselves from their background. To the extent that I could influence people, I wanted to avoid the mistakes we made in the aftermath of Vietnam.

During Operation Iraqi Freedom, I served as chaplain for the 4th Marine Division, the largest combat unit in the U.S. Marine Corps. As I counseled senior leaders on managing warriors' spiritual and emotional resilience, I drew on my experience in Vietnam. I advocated for programming and funds to support Marines, sailors, and their families. I showed them how inner battles require the same courage as urban warfare and hand-to-hand combat. I shared how the trauma of Vietnam still haunted me, even thirty years after returning home. I taught more than "history" … I taught them about *the past* from the perspective of someone who'd lived through it.

Those commanders listened intently and followed my advice to a tee. An older warrior's perspective spurred them to meaningful action —and they needed it, because the 4th Marines fought some of the fiercest battles of the War on Terror, including the Battle of Fallujah in 2004. They said "yes" to taking seriously the threat of spiritual and emotional fallout among their troops… and I believe it added strength to the "no" they delivered to the terrorists.

It goes to show how our pain, sorrows, or bad decisions are never "a waste" if we let the Spirit of God use them. Can you imagine, for just a moment, what kind of power *you* wield through your experiences? Have you thought about people in your life who could benefit from hearing your perspective? What if you suddenly said "yes" to facing the past—*your past*—and confronting it head-on? Could you also turn around and influence someone else for the better? Let me answer that by saying, "Yes – I've done it too many times for it to be a coincidence."

You've laid everything on the line, and whether leadership betrayed you or not is beside the point. Whatever mess you carry is now your *message*. Don't miss this moment. Find someone who can help you talk it through. You may not understand just yet… but if you carry the Hope of War, you have *all the hope you'll ever need*. God will supply the rest. You will always encounter younger, inexperienced warriors who need to hear your message.

May the words inscribed in this book serve as a timeless testimony to upholding truth, even when faced with opposition or the pressure to conform. I pray you remember – the truth dies when we stop defending it. But when we fight for truth, especially inside ourselves, it leads to lasting peace and joy. That, to me, is *The Hope of War*!

Acknowledgements

In the twilight of my years, one of my ambitions was to write a book capturing the memories of the people and events that forged a Christ-centered legacy filled with purpose and adventure. The biggest obstacle was getting started.

Therefore, I am forever indebted to my wife, Charlene, whose persistence convinced me of my obligation to document the journey that yielded hope against all odds. I appreciate the hours she spent reviewing each chapter, offering commentary and judgment, and ensuring clarity of thought.

I'm also indebted to my good friend and fellow Long Hollow Church Life Group member, Pat Lynch, who selflessly gave his time to read my manuscript during its developmental phase. Pat offered insights and interpretations from his combat experiences as a young Marine in Vietnam during the war's early years when the fighting was at its worst. His coaching helped me through those frustrating moments when I felt overwhelmed by the demands of the effort and on the verge of giving up. When undertaking anything significant, you need a friend to hold you accountable and to keep you moving forward to the next milestone.

I acknowledge my good friend, Stan E. Corvin, Jr., who unexpectedly went home to be with the Lord on January 25th, 2023. Stan served two combat tours in Vietnam as a helicopter pilot. God brings people into our lives at the right moment to help move us in a particular direction. Stan's encouragement helped me move beyond the reluctance to invest the time to share my legacy as a warrior and Navy chaplain. True friends say what needs to be said, even when inconvenient. Stan once told me, "You need to wise up, bub, and listen to Charlene about writing a book." I responded, "I'm still working on that." But Stan was right, and as Proverbs 27:9 says, "The wise counsel of a friend is as sweet as perfume and incense."

I also want to recognize Paul Edwards and Jason Todd, two exceptionally talented professionals at Emissary Publishing whose spiritual gifts, industry knowledge, and expertise helped me define the message I wanted to share with those willing to listen. Their input was critical in turning my rough draft into a focused and harmonious story and ensuring its relevance for this time in history.

I am also incredibly grateful to Ronnie and Francine Daniels, friends and fellow Life Group members at Long Hollow Church. Ron is a local entrepreneur and co-president of the Nashville Rose Society and Master Rosarian, instrumental in reviving and improving several high-profile Southern rose gardens. Ron is also the founder of Floral Ministry, an outreach program designed to connect others with a similar passion for growing and caring for roses. Ron and Francine were the ones who introduced me to Paul and Jason, and they graciously provided encouragement as my manuscript inched toward publication.

I'm grateful to Rear Admiral James McGarrah for devoting the time to write the foreword to my book. I served under Jim as battalion chaplain for Naval Mobile Construction Battalion Twenty-Four (Seabees) during Desert Shield and Desert Storm. In the aftermath, our paths crossed many times as we advanced through the ranks, facing new challenges and opportunities. Jim understands my struggle, perspective, and motivation better than most.

I'm also indebted to many friends who spent hours reviewing my manuscript before going to print. Most are retired Army and Navy chaplains and Navy and Marine Corps line officers who witnessed my story unfold in real-time. I treasure their expertise and insight, ensuring the story remains faithful to its purpose.

To you, the reader—thank you for taking the time to go back and walk with me through my journey. I pray you find what you were looking for. Remember, everyone wants to be considered a hero when there's no danger. That is why, in every generation, God seeks out those who honestly confess their weakness and are willing to rely on His strength to do what is impossible with the help of His intervention. Trust me, life offers no greater adventure than living according to God's plan and purpose.

Finally, I want to thank my family and friends who have stood with me through thick and thin throughout the years. Thank you for providing inspiration and encouragement for my life and ministry. Without you, I would never have discovered the extent of my calling or the power to imagine what could be.

About the Author

Larry D. Cripps was born near Smithville, TN. Drafted into the US Army in 1969, he served in the 11th Armored Cavalry Regiment in South Vietnam and Cambodia. During his 32 years of naval service, Larry served in various assignments including the U. S. Marine Corps, Combatant Commands, Naval Expeditionary Combat Command, and Naval Special Warfare Command. His military career and ministry spans three wars - Vietnam, Desert Shield and Desert Storm, the 9/11 Terrorist attacks, and the War on Terror. He attended the Naval Chaplain School, and holds a Bachelor of Arts in Biblical Education and History and a Masters of Divinity from Southwestern Baptist Theological Seminary. Larry and his wife, Charlene, reside in Hendersonville, TN.

Appendix

Chapter One

[1] "Free Records for Family Researching in DeKalb County Tennessee." Accessed November 17, 2023. https://genealogytrails.com/tenn/dekalb/

[2] "Tennessee in the American Civil War - Wikipedia." Accessed November 17, 2023. https://en.wikipedia.org/wiki/Tennessee_in_the_American_Civil_War.

[3] "William Brickly Stokes - Wikipedia." Accessed July 5, 2021.

[4] "5th Tennessee Cavalry Regiment (Union) - Wikipedia." Accessed November 17, 2023. https://en.wikipedia.org/wiki/5th_Tennessee_Cavalry_Regiment_(Union)

[5] "Exploring the Southern Tradition" (Abbeville Institute Press, 2019), 1328.

[6] Ibid.

[7] "Tennessee in the Great War, 1914 - 1918: A Guide to Collections at the Tennessee State Library and Archives | Tennessee Secretary of State." Accessed July 5, 2021. https://www.sos.tn.gov/products/tsla/tennessee-great-war-1914-1918-guide-collections-tennessee-state-library-and-archives

[8] Tennessee in World War II: A Guide to Collections at the Tennessee State Library and Archives | Tennessee Secretary of State." Accessed July 5, 2021. https://www.sos.tn.gov/products/tsla/tennessee-world-war-ii-guide-collections-tennessee-state-library-and-archives

[9] "Hidden Heroes of WWII: An Honor Roll for DeKalb County Women (Part I) – The Family History Librarian." Accessed July 5, 2021. https://thefamilyhistorylibrarian.com/2019/11/11/hidden-heroes-of-wwii-part1/

[10] "Breeds of Livestock - Holstein Cattle — Breeds of Livestock, Department of Animal Science." Accessed July 6, 2021. http://afs.okstate.edu/breeds/cattle/holstein

Chapter Two

[1] Erwin W. Lutzer, *No Reason to Hide* (Harvest House Publishing, Eugene, OR, 2022), 17.

[2] "Alexander the Great - *I Am Afraid of an Army lead by a Lion...*" Accessed November 20, 2023. https://www.brainyquote.com/quotes/alexander_the_great_391181

[3] Erwin W. Lutzer, *When A Nation Forgets God: 7 Lessons We Must Learn From Nazi Germany* (Moody Publishing, Chicago, IL, 2010), 121-122.

[4] "Harmony and Disruption: How 1960s Music Shaped the Societal Landscape - Brilliantio." Accessed November 22, 2023. https://brilliantio.com/how-did-1960s-music-affect-society/

[5] "1963: The Defining Year of the Civil Rights Movement | Race | The Guardian." Accessed November 18, 2023. https://www.theguardian.com/world/2013/may/07/1963-defining-year-civil-rights

[6] Ibid.

[7] Ibid.

[8] Ibid.

[9] "Ich Bin Ein Berliner - Wikipedia." Accessed November 18, 2023. https://en.wikipedia.org/wiki/Ich_bin_ein_Berliner

[10] "Reactions to the Assassination of John F. Kennedy - Wikipedia." Accessed November 18, 2023. https://en.wikipedia.org/wiki/Reactions_to_the_assassination_of_John_F._Kennedy

[11] Ibid.

[12] James Dobson, Life on the Edge: A Young Adult's Guide to A Meaningful Future, (World Publishing, 1995), 3.

Chapter Three

[1] In John's gospel, chapter 8, verse 32, Jesus says to his disciples, "You will know the truth, and the truth will set you free". The meaning of this verse is that by following Jesus' teachings and living according to his word, they will have a personal and experiential knowledge of the truth about God and themselves. This truth will liberate them from sin, ignorance, and bondage, and give them freedom and joy to serve God wherever He may lead. In other words, knowing the truth is a rock-steady way of life and the only dependable foundation for constructing one's life (see Psalm 26:3).

[2] "Quote by Sir Winston Churchill: 'To Each There Comes in Their Lifetime a Special...'" Accessed July 4, 2021. https://www.goodreads.com/quotes/67420-to-each-there-comes-in-their-lifetime-a-special-moment

[3] "Lyndon Johnson and the Great Society | US History II (OS Collection)." Accessed June 28, 2021. https://courses.lumenlearning.com/ushistory2os2xmaster/chapter/lyndon-johnson-and-the-great-society

[4] "Great Society - Programs, Definition & LBJ | HISTORY." Accessed November 22, 2023. https://www.history.com/topics/1960s/great-society

[5] "Voting Rights Act of 1965 - Definition, Summary & Significance | HISTORY." Accessed November 26, 2023. https://www.history.com/topics/black-history/voting-rights-act.

[6] "Lady Bird Johnson - Wikipedia." Accessed November 27, 2023. https://en.wikipedia.org/wiki/Lady_Bird_Johnson

[7] "8 Major Accomplishments Of Lyndon B Johnson - HRF." Accessed November 25, 2023. https://healthresearchfunding.org/8-major-accomplishments-of-lyndon-b-johnson/

[8] "LBJ's Medal for Valor 'was Sham' | World News | The Guardian." Accessed November 26, 2023. https://www.theguardian.com/world/2001/jul/06/internationaleducationnews.humanities

[9] "8 Major Accomplishments Of Lyndon B Johnson - HRF." Accessed November 25, 2023. https://healthresearchfunding.org/8-major-accomplishments-of-lyndon-b-johnson/

[10] "The Military Draft during the Vietnam War · Exhibit · Resistance and Revolution: The Anti- Vietnam War Movement at the University of Michigan, 1965-1972." Accessed November 23, 2023. https://michiganintheworld.history.lsa.umich.edu/antivietnamwar/exhibits/show/exhibit/draft_protests/the-military-draft-during-the-

[11] Ibid.

[12] "Tonkin Gulf Crisis, August 1964 - Summary." Accessed November 23, 2023. https://www.history.navy.mil/research/library/online-reading-room/title-list- alphabetically/t/tonkin-gulf-crisis/tonkin-gulf-crisis-aug-1964.html

[13] "Remembering Vietnam | National Archives." Accessed November 25, 2023. https://www.archives.gov/publications/prologue/2017/fall/remembering-vietnam

[14] "Ho Chi Minh Trail - Wikipedia." Accessed November 28, 2023. https://en.wikipedia.org/wiki/Ho_Chi_Minh_trail

[15] "Gulf of Tonkin Resolution - Wikipedia." Accessed November 28, 2023. https://en.wikipedia.org/wiki/Gulf_of_Tonkin_Resolution

[16] "The Military Draft During the Vietnam War · Exhibit · Resistance and Revolution: The Anti- Vietnam War Movement at the University of Michigan, 1965-1972." Accessed November 28, 2023.

¹⁷ "Robert Caro on the Art of Biography." Accessed November 29, 2023. https://www.robertcaro.org/post/robert-caro-on-the-art-of-biography

¹⁸ H. R. McMasters, *Dereliction of Duty* (HarperCollins Publishers, New York, 1998), 270.

¹⁹ "AIR FORCE Magazine," 2011.

²⁰ "Conscription in the United States - Wikipedia." Accessed November 28, 2023. https://en.wikipedia.org/wiki/Conscription_in_the_United_States

²¹ "The American Soldier in Vietnam | Encyclopedia.Com." Accessed June 18, 2021. https://www.encyclopedia.com/history/encyclopedias-almanacs-transcripts-and-maps/American-soldier-vietnam

²² The Military Draft During the Vietnam War · Exhibit · Resistance and Revolution: The Anti- Vietnam War Movement at the University of Michigan, 1965-1972." Accessed November 28, 2023.

²³ James Garfield, "A Century of Congress," *Atlantic*, July 1877, 63,64.

Chapter Four

¹ Michael Lind, *Vietnam The Necessary War: A Reinterpretation of America's Most Disastrous Military Conflict* (A Touchstone Book Published by Simon and Schuster, 1999), 1.

² Ibid.

³ "Vietnam War - Diem Regime, Viet Cong, Conflict | Britannica." Accessed December 1, 2023. https://www.britannica.com/event/Vietnam-War/The-Diem-regime-and-the-Viet-Cong

4 "Nixon's Retrospective on the Vietnam War – The Diplomat." Accessed December 2, 2023. https://thediplomat.com/2015/04/nixons-retrospective-on-the-vietnam-war

5 "As President, John F. Kennedy Faced Challenges of Fast-Changing World – Catholic Philly." Accessed December 1, 2023. https://catholicphilly.com/2013/11/features/jfk-features/as-president-john-f-kennedy-faced-challenges-of-fast-changing-world

6 Vietnam War - Diem Regime, Viet Cong, Conflict | Britannica." Accessed December 1, 2023. https://www.britannica.com/event/Vietnam-War/The-Diem-regime-and-the-Viet-Cong

7 Ibid.

8 Ibid.

9 Ibid.

10 Ibid.

11 Ibid.

12 "Vietnam Battlefield Tours - Corps Tactical Zones." Accessed March 1, 2022. https://www.vietnambattlefieldtours.com/tours/ctz/zones.asp

13 Jack Shulimson, U. S. Marines in Vietnam-An Expanding War in 1966 (History and Museums Division, Washington, D. C., 1982), 8.

Chapter Five

1 John C. Maxwell, *Learning from the Giants* (Faith Words, Hachette Book Group, New York, 2014), 9, 10.

2 Aleksandr Solzhenitsyn, *A World Split Apart* (New York: Harper & Row, 1978), 61,111.

3 "Vietnam War - De-Escalation, Negotiation, Vietnamization |
Britannica." Accessed December 2, 2023.

4 "Fifty Years Ago, a Rag-Tag Group of Acid-Dropping Activists Tried
to 'Levitate' the Pentagon | At the Smithsonian| Smithsonian
Magazine." Accessed December 6, 2023. https://
www.smithsonianmag.com/smithsonian-institution/how-rag-tag-
group-acid-dropping-activists-tried-levitate-pentagon-180965338

5 "Khe Sanh - Location, Vietnam War & Who Won." Accessed
December 6, 2023. https://www.history.com/topics/vietnam-war/
battle-of-khe-sanh-1

6 "Tet Offensive | Facts, Casualties, Videos, & Significance |
Britannica." Accessed December 7, 2023. https://www.britannica.com/
topic/Tet-Offensive

7 Ibid.

8 "Robert McNamara - Wikipedia." Accessed December 7, 2023.
https://en.wikipedia.org/wiki/Robert_McNamara#cite_note-
FOOTNOTELangguth2000446-137

9 Tet Offensive | Facts, Casualties, Videos, & Significance |
Britannica." Accessed December 7, 2023. https://www.britannica.com/
topic/Tet-Offensive

10 Ibid.

11 "How the Tet Offensive Shocked Americans into Questioning If the
Vietnam War Could Be Won | HISTORY." Accessed December 6,
2023. https://www.history.com/news/tet-offensive-1968-vietnam-war-
surprise-attack-changed-american-public-opinion

12 "101st Airborne Division Arrives in Vietnam | July 29, 1965 |
HISTORY." Accessed December 10, 2023. https://www.history.com/
this-day-in-history/101st-airborne-division-arrives-in-vietnam

13 "Bloody 10-Day Battle at 'Hamburger Hill' Begins." Accessed December 10, 2023. https://www.history.com/this-day-in-history/paratroopers-battle-for-hamburger-hill
14 "William Westmoreland." Accessed December 10, 2023. https://www.history.com/topics/vietnam-war/william-westmoreland

Chapter Six

1 "The Vietnam War's Effect on Nixon's 1968 Win - The History Reader: The History Reader." Accessed December 11, 2023.

2 Ibid.

3 Ibid.

4 Lewis Sorely, *A Better War: The Unexamined Victories and Final Tragedy of America's Last Years in Vietnam* (Harcourt Brace & Company, New York, 1999), XVI.

5 "Creighton Abrams - Citizendium." Accessed December 13, 2023. https://en.citizendium.org/wiki/Creighton_Abrams

6 "Vietnamization | Encyclopedia.Com." Accessed December 13, 2023. https://www.encyclopedia.com/history/dictionaries-thesauruses-pictures-and-press-releases/vietnamization

7 "Battle of Huế - Wikipedia." Accessed December 13, 2023. https://en.wikipedia.org/wiki/Battle_of_Hue

8 "Jesus Movement - Wikipedia." Accessed December 17, 2023. https://en.wikipedia.org/wiki/Jesus_movement

9 Ibid.

10 "2023 Asbury Revival - Wikipedia." Accessed December 17, 2023. https://en.wikipedia.org/wiki/2023_Asbury_revival

Chapter Seven

[1] "How the 'Horse Soldiers' Helped Liberate Afghanistan from the Taliban 18 Years Ago." Accessed December 21, 2023. https://www.militarytimes.com/news/your-military/2019/10/18/how-the-horse-soldiers-helped-liberate-afghanistan-from-the-taliban-18-years-ago

[2] Ibid.

[3] "Vietnam War - De-Escalation, Negotiation, Vietnamization | Britannica." Accessed December 21, 2023. https://www.britannica.com/event/Vietnam-War/De-escalation-negotiation-and-Vietnamization

[4] Ibid.

[5] Ibid.

[6] Ibid.

[7] "First Stop To Vietnam, The Induction Center." Accessed December 20, 2023. https://www.historynet.com/first-stop-vietnam-induction-center

[8] "An Overview of the US Army Drill Sergeant – Boot Camp & Military Fitness Institute." Accessed October 14, 2022. https://bootcampmilitaryfitnessinstitute.com/militarytraining/armed-forces-of-the-united-states-of-america/us-military-training-overview/anoverview-of-the-us-army-drill-sergeant

Chapter Eight

[1] John C. Maxwell, *Learning from the Giants* (FaithWords, Hachette Book Group, New York, NY, 2014), 41.

2 "Nixon and Congress: A Very Spotty Record - The New York Times." Accessed January 17, 2023. https://www.nytimes.com/1970/09/13/archives/nixon-and-congress-a-very-spottyrecord.html

3 Ibid.

4 "Milestones: 1969–1976 - Office of the Historian." Accessed January 29, 2023. https://history.state.gov/milestones/1969-1976/ending-vietnam

5 "Henry Kissinger Begins Secret Negotiations with North Vietnamese - HISTORY." Accessed January 31, 2023. https://www.history.com/this-day-in-history/kissinger-begins-secret-negotiations-with-north-vietnamese

6 "The Paris Peace Accords in 1973: Nixon, Kissinger & North Vietnam - Video & Lesson Transcript | Study.Com." Accessed January 30, 2023. https://study.com/academy/lesson/theparis-peace-accords-in-1973-nixon-kissinger-north-vietnam.html

7 "President Nixon's Speech on 'Vietnamization,' November 3, 1969 - The Wars for Viet Nam - Vassar College." Accessed January 30, 2023. https://www.vassar.edu/vietnam/documents/doc14.html

8 Ibid.

9 Ibid.

10 Ibid.

11 Intelligence Message by the Secretary of State with Subject Line: Nanoi's Angry Reaction to President's Speech, dated November 6, 1969

12 "When Nixon Visited China—And Changed the Balance of Cold War Power - HISTORY." Accessed February 1, 2023. https://www.history.com/news/nixon-china-visit-cold-war

13 "President Nixon's Speech on 'Vietnamization,' November 3, 1969 - The Wars for Viet Nam - Vassar College." Accessed January 30, 2023

14 Ibid.

15 "About Li Po | Academy of American Poets." Accessed December 27, 2023. https://poets.org/poet/li-po

Chapter Nine

1 "How Nixon's Invasion of Cambodia Triggered a Check on Presidential Power - HISTORY." Accessed January 14, 2023. https://www.history.com/news/nixon-war-powers-act-vietnam-war

2 John M. Shaw, *The Cambodian Campaign: The 1970 Offensive and America's Vietnam War,* (University Press of Kansas, Lawrence Kansas, 2005), 154.

Chapter Ten

1 "This General Challenged the President and Saved American Lives." Accessed December 30, 2023. https://www.militarytimes.com/military-honor/salute-veterans/2017/11/02/this-general-challenged-the-president-and-saved-american-lives

2 "How Nixon's Invasion of Cambodia Triggered a Check on Presidential Power | HISTORY." Accessed December 30, 2023. https://www.history.com/news/nixon-war-powers-act-vietnam-war-cambodia

3 "How Nixon's Invasion of Cambodia Triggered a Check on Presidential Power | HISTORY." Accessed December 30, 2023. https://www.history.com/news/nixon-war-powers-act-vietnam-war-cambodia

4 Donald Snedeker, *The Blackhorse In Vietnam: The 11th Armored Cavalry Regiment in Vietnam and Cambodia, 1966-1972* (Casemate Publishers, Havertown, PA, 2020), 170

5 "1972 Election | 50th Anniversary of the Historic Landslide Election." Accessed December 31, 2023. https://www.nixonfoundation.org/2022/11/50th-anniversary-historic-landslide-election-1972

Chapter Twelve

1 "The Great Communicator: The Political Rhetoric of Ronald Reagan (Part 1) - Intercollegiate Studies Institute." Accessed January 9, 2024. https://isi.org/intercollegiate-review/the-great-communicator-the-political-rhetoric-of-ronald-reagan-part-1

2 Ibid.

3 Ibid.

4 "How Ronald Reagan Won the Cold War | The Heritage Foundation." Accessed January 15, 2024. https://www.heritage.org/conservatism/commentary/how-ronald-reagan-won-the-cold-war

5 Joseph Stanik, *"Twilight of the Cold War: Contraction, Reform, and Revival," in James Bradford, ed., America, Seapower, and the World* (West Sussex, UK: John Wiley & Sons, 2016), 312.

6 Stanik, *"Twilight of the Cold War,"* 312.

7 John Lehman, "Is Naval Aviation Culture Dead?" U.S. Naval Institute: *Proceedings* 137, no. 9 (September 2011).

8 26. Stanik, *Twilight of the Cold War*, 316.

9 Stanik, *Twilight of the Cold War*, 317.

10 Stanik, *Twilight of the Cold War*, 320.